GameSalad
Beginner's Guide

A fun, quick, step-by-step guide to creating games with levels, physics, sound, and numerous enemies using GameSalad

Miguel DeQuadros

BIRMINGHAM - MUMBAI

GameSalad
Beginner's Guide

First published: March 2012

Production Reference: 1050312

Published by Packt Publishing Ltd.
Livery Place
35 Livery Street
Birmingham B3 2PB, UK.

ISBN 978-1-84969-220-5

www.packtpub.com

Cover Image by Miguel DeQuadros (miguel@wurdindustries.com)

Credits

Author

Miguel DeQuadros

Reviewers

Dick A. Lou

Craig Pearson

Acquisition Editor

Rashmi Phadnis

Lead Technical Editor

Susmita Panda

Technical Editor

Vishal D'souza

Copy Editor

Laxmi Subramanian

Project Coordinator

Kushal Bhardwaj

Proofreader

Dan McMahon

Indexer

Monica Ajmera Mehta

Graphics

Manu Joseph

Production Coordinator

Prachali Bhiwandkar

Cover Work

Prachali Bhiwandkar

About the Author

Miguel DeQuadros is a Game Developer and founder of the independent development studio Wurd Industries, based in Ontario, Canada. He has been developing iPhone games since the release of the App Store back at the exciting release of iOS 2.0. Since then, working under Wurd Industries, he has had eight games and one entertainment app published world-wide on the App Store, with more to come.

Originally interested in 3D animation and graphic design, Miguel focused mainly on this, but then got the game development "bug" and has been developing iPhone Apps since 2008. This allows him to use his creativity and knowledge of 3D animation for cut scenes and videos within his apps, and he loves every minute of it. Starting from his first project "Toy Tennis" back in 2008 (which, to this day, still remains a very popular app, thought it has been updated quite a bit with new graphics and social integration), down to his current project iMMUNE 3: The Final Stand, he continues to develop iPhone apps.

He began expressing interest in GameSalad when it was first launched in March 2009, but never started using it until January of 2010, when he started to develop his third iOS game, iMMUNE 2: Rise of the Salmonella, a 2D platformer sequel to the iMMUNE series. To this day, he and Wurd Industries continue to be Professional Members of the GameSalad community and still use GameSalad for prototyping and developing games for the iOS devices, and are now branching out to Mac development.

I would like to thank my dad John, my brother, and sister in-law Johnny and Katie, my cousin Corey, my best friends Brandon and Kaleb, and a very special thanks to my wonderful fiance Joanne for encouraging me during the writing of this book and spending countless hours on the phone with me. There are many other of my friends who were very encouraging to me and I thank you for the constant boost of confidence. Without you guys I don't think I could have done this book by myself. I would also like to thank Packt Publishing, and all the wonderful employees who helped me out, both in the initial stages and into the final chapters of the book. Your professionalism and ability to clearly explain things also helped me a lot, thank you Rashmi Phadnis, Srimoyee Ghosal, Kushal Bhardwaj, Priya Mukherji, Vishal D'souza, Hyacintha D'souza, and Newton Sequeira for everything. You made the production of this book a very smooth process.

About the Reviewers

Dick Abanto Lou was born in Trujillo, Perú and is currently the CEO of Gamitz Mobile Studios and Dekoders In Vitro Studios, both being independent videogame-related startups located in Venezuela.

Videogames are his passion and daily bread, that's why he decided not to only play them but also to create them. So, he founded Gamitz Mobile Studios. His first game went directly to the iOS platforms called "El Gocho" and had a decent success within the Venezuelan App store, reaching the top 5 in all free apps in just a week.

His knowledge enabled him to make "El Gocho" a board game, similar to peg solitaire, which was a challenging task as GameSalad doesn't provide any reference in how to make board games.

"El Gocho" had gained the attention of many locals, but the most important fact of the game is to give hope to all the people who want to make videogames, as this is something really hard to accomplish due to the circumstances in Venezuela.

Besides his work as a videogame developer and CEO at Gamitz Mobile Studios, he founded a company called Dekoders In Vitro Studios that will encourage, help, and teach people in Latin America to make videogames with a very wide range of available tools, from open source projects to elite high cost platforms, and also publish them.

Craig Pearson (aka single sparq) has been an independent Game Developer for 3 years but has played games for more than 35 years. As an avid Apple fan, Craig previously ran two Apple-centric websites and since then has focused more on being an iOS developer in his spare time.

Without formal training, Craig has accumulated experience in all media areas such as video (editing, directing, and writing), Web development (CSS, HTML, and PHP), art direction (Photoshop, Illustrator, and Quark/InDesign) and music (Keyboard, Logic Pro, and Garageband).

Before finding the ultimate outlet of utilizing these skills in game development, Craig wrote and produced the album TwoPointZero, under the moniker of Monospark, currently available in iTunes.

Games produced with GameSalad include Space Tech Defender, Orbitz Jump Adventure, Barnyard Stackem, and Suburban Grand Prix.

When not making games, or enjoying life with his wife and daughter, Craig is the Manager of web development for a Canadian magazine publisher, managing over 40 Joomla-based websites.

Thanks to the author for the opportunity to be a part of this book and to GameSalad for the software that even a non-coder like me can use. To Apple for the tools to be so creative in so many ways. Also, a big thanks to Kathy and Natasha for allowing me the time to fulfill my passions.

www.PacktPub.com

Support files, eBooks, discount offers and more

You might want to visit www.PacktPub.com for support files and downloads related to your book.

Did you know that Packt offers eBook versions of every book published, with PDF and ePub files available? You can upgrade to the eBook version at www.PacktPub.com and as a print book customer, you are entitled to a discount on the eBook copy. Get in touch with us at service@packtpub.com for more details.

At www.PacktPub.com, you can also read a collection of free technical articles, sign up for a range of free newsletters and receive exclusive discounts and offers on Packt books and eBooks.

http://PacktLib.PacktPub.com

Do you need instant solutions to your IT questions? PacktLib is Packt's online digital book library. Here, you can access, read and search across Packt's entire library of books.

Why Subscribe?

- Fully searchable across every book published by Packt
- Copy and paste, print and bookmark content
- On demand and accessible via web browser

Free Access for Packt account holders

If you have an account with Packt at www.PacktPub.com, you can use this to access PacktLib today and view nine entirely free books. Simply use your login credentials for immediate access.

Table of Contents

Preface

In July 2008, Apple revolutionized mobile entertainment. They brought us the App Store. This was not only incredible for those who owned "iDevices" (iPod Touch, iPhone, and so on), who could now download apps and games to make their device even more entertaining, but it opened up a new scope for developers. The incredible new technology of the iPhone and iPod Touch made it possible for developers to create apps and games in which they could incorporate multi-touch controls, make use of the accelerometer and even allow the user's music to be played in-game. To date, the Apple App Store has over 425,000 apps available worldwide, and Apple has paid out billions of dollars to developers.

Apple also made it easy for individuals to become developers; anyone with programming knowledge and a Mac could become a developer, create apps and have their creation released around the world. The SDK (XCode) gave users the ability to create visually using the Interface Builder, and code everything within a uniform software development kit.

If you are like almost everyone else in the world, you don't know any programming language, nor do you have the time to sit down and learn one. That's where GameSalad comes in. What is GameSalad you ask? GameSalad is a fantastic, powerful creation tool that allows you to develop iPhone games! The best part about it is there is no programming involved whatsoever! With a simple drag-and-drop user interface, and behavior-based development, putting together an awesome game has never been easier! It is possible to create a fully playable game in less than half an hour! This book is going to cover the ins and outs of game development, sprite creation, planning, and all you need to know about GameSalad.

What this book covers

Chapter 1, You Need A Plan!, teaches you the basics of planning a game. You will learn how to think of an original idea, use storyboards, and create design documents, which will streamline your development phase by planning your game.

Chapter 2, Getting Started with GameSalad, guides you through GameSalad's user interface, creating a new project, working with actors and adding simple controls to a game.

Chapter 3, Add Zest to your Salad, teaches you how to create sprites (or images) for your game. Then we will import those images and some sound effects to add some more "zest" to our games.

Chapter 4, Starting Simple: Ball Drop Part 1, starts you off by creating a fully-fledged game, with physics, a menu system, and touch controls.

Chapter 5, Starting Simple: Ball Drop Part 2, continues the creation of our ball drop game. By the end of this chapter, you will have created your first game in GameSalad!

Chapter 6, Space Defender Part 1, creates an Asteroids clone. We are going to create a good user interface, create smart enemies, and more!

Chapter 7, Space Defender Part 2, completes our Asteroids clone by setting up Game Center leaderboards. We will also test our game on our iOS device.

Chapter 8, Metal Mech Part 1, explains the creation of a large game that will have multiple large levels, make full use of the iOS (can also be used for Android publishing) accelerometer, and intelligent AI. In this chapter, we are going to create our user interface, smart enemies that will detect you as you approach, and button/accelerometer controls.

Chapter 9, Metal Mech Part 2, continues to work on our Mech game. In this chapter we are will add sound effects, particle explosions, jet trails and smoking, burning wreckage.

Chapter 10, Metal Mech Part 3, covers the creation of our level bounds (so the player can't walk through obstacles), turrets, weapon overheating, scoring, mission briefing (for a cool-looking User Interface!) and we are going to create the accelerometer controls!

Chapter 11, Metal Mech Part 4, teaches us to prepare our game for the iOS App Store. We will create iAds for extra revenue, Game Center Leaderboards, and we will deploy our app on to our device for testing. Then, we will upload our game to the App Store.

Appendix A, Getting Started in iDevelopment, covers the technical aspect of iOS development. We will discuss creating a developer account, provisioning profiles, installing Xcode and the iOS SDK, and more.

What you need for this book

The following are necessary for designing a game in GameSalad:

- ◆ You will need an Intel-based Mac running Mac OS X 10.6 Snow Leopard or higher.
- ◆ GameSalad Creator with a registered account, free or paid (either is okay for development, it is not mandatory to have a paid account. We will discuss this in the book).
- ◆ A registered Apple Developer account (we will discuss in this book).
- ◆ Internet access (for getting images, deploying your app, and so on).
- ◆ An imaging program: Gimp, Pixelmator, Photoshop, or any equivalent.
- ◆ Optional: 3D Modeling tools, such as 3DS Max, Maya, or Blender3D.
- ◆ Optional: A graphics tablet that will make it much easier to draw sprites.

Who this book is for

Anyone who has ever dreamed about creating games and making money off them, this book is for you! It is also for all those who are neither familiar with programming, nor want to take the time to learn a language (let's face it, not too many people have the time to learn a programming language).

Conventions

In this book, you will find several headings appearing frequently.

To give clear instructions of how to complete a procedure or task, we use:

Time for action – heading

1. Action 1
2. Action 2
3. Action 3

Instructions often need some extra explanation so that they make sense, so they are followed with:

What just happened?

This heading explains the working of tasks or instructions that you have just completed.

You will also find some other learning aids in the book, including:

Pop quiz – heading

These are short multiple choice questions intended to help you test your own understanding.

Have a go hero – heading

These set practical challenges and give you ideas for experimenting with what you have learned.

You will also find a number of styles of text that distinguish between different kinds of information. Here are some examples of these styles, and an explanation of their meaning.

Code words in text are shown as follows: "That is just for moving the character, then you have to set up timers for the game, and an NSMutableArray for the character animation."

A block of code is set as follows:

```
-(void)walk_left {
  character.center = CGPointMake (character.center.x - 10,
  character.center.y);
}"
```

New terms and **important words** are shown in bold. Words that you see on the screen, in menus or dialog boxes for example, appear in the text like this: "Click the **Download Free App – GameSalad Creator** button".

 Warnings or important notes appear in a box like this.

 Tips and tricks appear like this.

Reader feedback

Feedback from our readers is always welcome. Let us know what you think about this book—what you liked or may have disliked. Reader feedback is important for us to develop titles that you really get the most out of.

To send us general feedback, simply send an e-mail to feedback@packtpub.com, and mention the book title through the subject of your message.

If there is a topic that you have expertise in and you are interested in either writing or contributing to a book, see our author guide on www.packtpub.com/authors.

Customer support

Now that you are the proud owner of a Packt book, we have a number of things to help you to get the most from your purchase.

Downloading the support files

You can download the example files for all Packt books you have purchased from your account at http://www.packtpub.com. The colored images for this book can be downloaded from http://www.packtpub.com/sites/default/files/downloads/2205_Images.pdf. If you purchased this book elsewhere, you can visit http://www.packtpub.com/support and register to have the files e-mailed directly to you.

Errata

Although we have taken every care to ensure the accuracy of our content, mistakes do happen. If you find a mistake in one of our books—maybe a mistake in the text or the code—we would be grateful if you would report this to us. By doing so, you can save other readers from frustration and help us improve subsequent versions of this book. If you find any errata, please report them by visiting http://www.packtpub.com/support, selecting your book, clicking on the **errata submission form** link, and entering the details of your errata. Once your errata are verified, your submission will be accepted and the errata will be uploaded to our website, or added to any list of existing errata, under the Errata section of that title.

Piracy

Piracy of copyright material on the Internet is an ongoing problem across all media. At Packt, we take the protection of our copyright and licenses very seriously. If you come across any illegal copies of our works, in any form, on the Internet, please provide us with the location address or website name immediately so that we can pursue a remedy.

Please contact us at copyright@packtpub.com with a link to the suspected pirated material.

We appreciate your help in protecting our authors, and our ability to bring you valuable content.

Questions

You can contact us at questions@packtpub.com if you are having a problem with any aspect of the book, and we will do our best to address it.

1
You Need a Plan!

Game development is a wonderful and enjoyable pastime, from the thrill of getting the creative juices flowing, through writing ideas down on paper, to seeing those ideas go from paper to the screen and into a game engine. Finally, seeing the product spread throughout the world and achieving fame for the game is a feeling like no other. Many people, however, do not consider what is involved in creating a game. The first step is planning your game, writing up documentation describing it, drawing up levels, and more. Having your game planned before you start developing improves the fluidity of creation. Believe me, a retail game on a console did not just happen, a developer wasn't sitting at his computer and started creating, no! Creative teams designed the game in all its details. Mind you, you do not have to go into such detail, but writing down a rough idea will surely ease your game's development. It can also be a lot of fun designing your game; once you get started, the ideas will come very quickly and you'll be on a roll. It doesn't matter where in your design document you start, it can be a simple character sketch, or a really cool level design; once you get started, it will all come together. Let me demonstrate how easy it is. Let's say, for example, your main character's name is Maximus, the son of a Roman Centurion. One night, his father leaves the house to get him a meal. Hours later, he has not returned. Maximus ventures forth, and soon finds out that his father was captured by the evil Druid Seraphix. Now things are coming together aren't they? See from there, now you have a baseline, you know what your player has to do, and filling in the details will come easily. Let's say, your first mission is to enter into Druid's hideout to save your father, but before you enter the dungeon the Druid finds you, and sends you to a faraway land. Now, you have to fight your way back to the hideout. As you do, you get stronger and better equipment. See, it's easy!

In this chapter, we are going to consider the following:

◆ How to come up with an original idea for a game

◆ Design documents (what your character will do, who he will fight, and so on)

◆ Creating Storyboards and Levels

Make sure you have some time, some peace, and a quiet environment, so you can think, and if necessary, an extra-large coffee or latte from your favorite cafe.

First, let's see how to come up with an **original idea**.

How to come up with an original idea

Today, there are literally millions of games available, from gaming consoles to mobile platforms. They range from realistic simulation racing games, to story-driven role-playing games. With so many games out there, you might think that coming up with an original idea would be difficult, and it can be. Simple games are often the most fun (and highest-grossing) for mobile platforms. Take for example, one of the highest-grossing iOS game, Angry Birds. The game is not complex, the story is quite simple and yet it has hit it big. Why? It's a simple game, with easy addictive gameplay, a game that will keep the user coming back to play it. It's one of those games that when someone downloads, they will go to their friends and say, "*Hey have you seen this game? It's so addictive!*"

Your idea may not be 100 percent original, but you can make it unique. Games that take place after the apocalypse or where you have to save the world by killing countless aliens hordes are a dime a dozen. And as fun as these games can be, they lack originality. The key to creating an original idea is to do your research, look at the store shelves and see the same genre over and over again, then break the mould, be original my friend! You can even mix and match certain game elements from different genres, first person shooter + puzzle = Portal, RPG + Third Person Shooter = Mass Effect. These are all ingenious ideas, and games that were very successful.

Another good piece of advice is to look around, look at your surroundings. See any good game ideas? Are you near a lake? How about a scuba diver game? Or a submarine game? Have you ever had a bat or a bird enter your house? Play a garbage man collecting garbage being thrown from buildings. The original ideas are endless, and are usually right in front of your face. Also, you can look at classic games—released many years ago—that have been long forgotten, on the Atari, NES, Commodore 64, and so on. Original ideas that have been forgotten are endless.

Design documentation

Ok, so now you have your idea all ready, it's time to get it all on paper, or if you like on your computer. What's included in the design documentation? Simply, everything! What is the name of your character? What will he do? What will he look like? Who will he fight? What weapons or items will he use? And so on.

Following is an example of a design document:

1. Game Name
2. Game Concept
3. Features
4. Genre
5. Target Audience
6. Game Flow Summary - How does the player move through the game.
7. Look and feel - What is the basic look and feel of the game? What is visual style?
8. Project Scope - A Summary of the scope of the game.
9. Number of levels
10. Number of NPC's (Non Player Characters)
11. Number of weapons
12. Game Progression
13. Mission/challenge Structure
14. Puzzle Structure
15. Objectives - What are the objectives of the game?
16. Physics - How does the physical universe work?
17. Movements
18. Objects
19. Picking Up Objects
20. Moving Objects
21. Actions
22. Switches and Buttons
23. Picking Up, Carrying and Dropping
24. Talking
25. Reading
26. Combat
27. Cheats and Easter Eggs
28. Pilot
29. Game World Details
30. Characters
    1. Player
        1. Back Story
        2. Personality
        3. Look
        4. Special Abilities
        5. Relevance to game story
31. Level #1
    1. Synopsis
    2. Introductory Material (Mission briefing if needed)
    3. Objectives
    4. Physical Description
    5. Map
    6. Level Walkthrough
    7. Closing Material (Mission Debriefing)
32. etc.
    1. HUD - What controls
    2. Menus
33. Control System - How does the game player control the game? What are the specific commands?
34. Music
35. Enemy AI - Villains and Monsters
36. Non-combat Characters
37. Friendly Characters
38. Support AI
39. Target Hardware (iphone, or ipad)
40. Concept Art
41. Characters
42. Environments
43. Equipment
44. Art

Get the idea? This level of detail is not needed for your game, unless you absolutely want to. Let's get a stripped down, easier to use, less headache-inducing template, shall we?

◆ Name of your game

◆ Features (What would you like in your game, Game Center, leaderboards, and so on)

◆ Story of your game

◆ Look and feel (Describe an art style you would like for your game, that is, dark, gritty, cartoon, and so on)

◆ Targeted number of levels

◆ Weapon types (If designing a shooting or an action game)

◆ Game progression (How the game is going to play out, for example, what will happen to your character once he finds the hidden scepter? How will the storyline change?)

◆ Objectives of the game (Things your player will have to complete to beat the game)

◆ Movement (How will your player move, 2D side-scroller? Bird's eye view?)

◆ Objects (What will your player collect? Coins for points? Hearts for health? Glowing orbs for ammo?)

◆ Player characteristics (What's his name? What can he do? What special abilities does he have or will he gain? What's his story? Where will he go after your game?)

◆ Hidden game features (What will you hide in the game as easter eggs, if any)

◆ Combat (How will players fight? Shooting? Hand to hand? Death by Tofu?)

◆ Main menu design (What is your menu screen going to look like? Background image? Buttons? Copyright information?)

◆ Game controls (Onscreen buttons or joysticks? Accelerometer movement?)

◆ NPCs (Important Non-Player Characters that will be seen in the game)

◆ Enemy's characteristics (self-explanatory, but how can they be defeated? How can you be hurt by them?)

◆ Game HUD (The overall look of the in-game heads up display, what will it show? Score? Health? Ammo?)

That's easier now, isn't it? Including this information will certainly ease development, as knowing everything when you get into the game will make designing the characters, levels, and more much quicker. Now that you have the design documentation done, let's get started on the level design, and storyboards.

Storyboards and Level Design

Storyboards are useful for in-game cutscenes. Storyboards are graphic organizers such as a series of images displayed in sequence for the purpose of pre-visualizing a cut scene. This process was invented by Walt Disney in the 1930s, and has been adopted by animation studios around the world. Following is an example of what a **storyboard for a game** looks like:

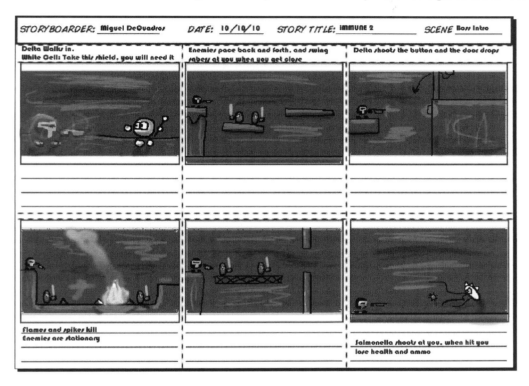

Now that you have an idea of what a storyboard looks like, you can create your own. You do not need to create one if you aren't doing any cutscenes in your game, though they can help with level design too.

Take a look at the resources section of this book; you will find a download link for the empty storyboard template.

Downloading the support files

You can download the example files for all Packt books you have purchased from your account at `http://www.packtpub.com`. The colored images for this book can be downloaded from `http://www.packtpub.com/sites/default/files/downloads/2205_Images.pdf`. If you purchased this book elsewhere, you can visit `http://www.packtpub.com/support` and register to have the files e-mailed directly to you.

You can draw a rough sketch of each frame in the boxes, and write a dialogue or any special instruction—such as "*Character moves to left past screen*"—on the lines.

Level design is also very important for the creation of your game. Designing levels in advance makes it easier to create them within your game engine. When you draw level design templates, they should include every detail, such as locations of collectables, enemies, and so on. A good 2D platformer level is not linear, meaning it's not straightforward. It involves jumping and climbing over obstacles, alternate paths to get across that big chasm preventing you from reaching your goal, and various other challenges; but even if you are creating a table tennis game, or a racing game, it's still a good idea to design your level/scene before you implement it within the game engine Let's take a look at a sample level design sheet for a platform game:

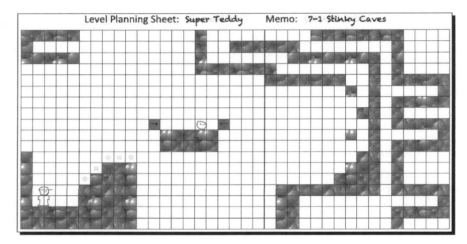

Following is another example of a level design sheet:

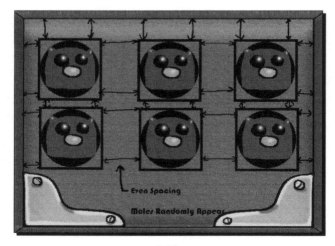

As you can see, this level design sheet can be very handy when it comes to designing a rough copy of your level; it will make development much easier. Once it's all planned, it will take very little time to implement it in your game engine. It can show you where you are going to start your character, where certain collectables are going to be, where your enemies will be, where the invisible collider "walls" will be—so that your enemies won't fall off the platform, and even hidden areas in which you will find secret collectables and hidden ways to get there—such as hidden updrafts that will throw your character up to a secret hole in the wall to collect the special coin.

As with the storyboard template, you can find this template in the resources section of this book. Print out a couple of these pages, and put them in a binder. It's a great idea to have your own special binder specifically for your game design. Being organized is a good idea when planning your game, finding things is so much easier when you don't have to search the pile of papers on your desk.

When you get into it, designing and planning your game can be very much fun, especially when you get on a roll and the creative juices start flowing. It can take minutes, or many days, to think of a good working idea for a game, but once you have that idea and build on it, it can become a design to be proud of and want to show off the finished product.

Do you have your game planned out yet? No? Well that's okay, for the rest of this book the games are designed for you; you just have to put them all together. If you do have your game all planned out, what we are going to consider in this book will help you get started with developing it. It's going to be a wild ride... Want to get a good idea of what we are going to accomplish in this book? Following are a few screenshots just to whet your appetite.

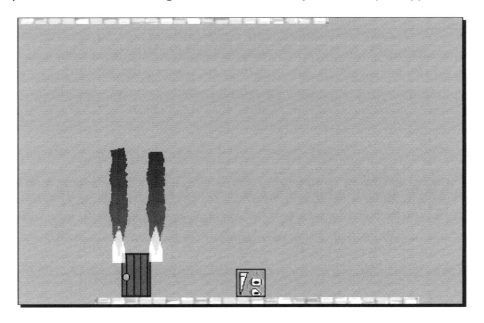

This game is a fun platform game that will teach us about physics, platform movement, and particles.

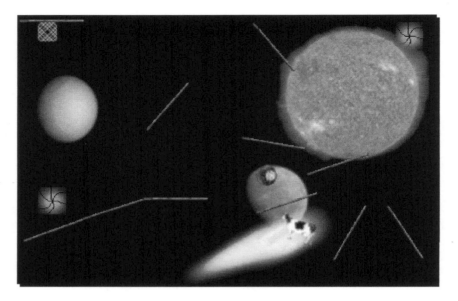

Everything looks pretty cool huh? The following is the last screenshot in this section, it's an asteroid clone that we are going to make!

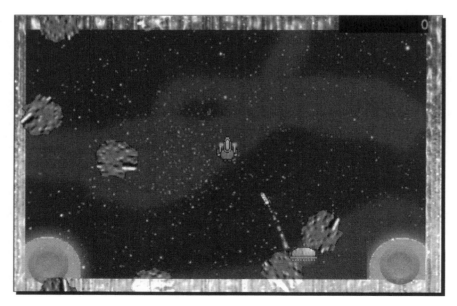

Now, let's have a quiz to see what you have learned.

Pop quiz

1. What are the top selling mobile games?

    a. Shoot 'em ups.

    b. Racing games.

    c. Simple games with addictive gameplay.

    d. None of the above.

2. Why is it a good idea to have a design document?

    a. It's not.

    b. It's good to have in case your idea gets questioned.

    c. Helps with publishing your game.

    d. Improves the work flow, allowing easy reference.

3. Who started using storyboards?

    a. Walt Disney.

    b. Pixar.

    c. Lucasfilm.

    d. Warner Brothers.

Summary

In this chapter, we got some tips on how to think of an original idea for your game, and how to create a design document, storyboards, and level design templates.

Using storyboard and level design templates, we learned that we can improve your development time by having everything planned out, allowing quick easy reference when implementing your design within the game engine. The design documents help considerably when designing your characters and developing your game, you already have all your ideas written down, so all you have to do is put them together in your engine. Speaking of game engines, in the next chapter, we are going to get started with GameSalad—a super easy engine—which allows you to create awesome games for iOS (iPhone, iPod Touch, and iPad) quickly and easily with absolutely no programming!

2
Getting Started with GameSalad

So, you're ready to become an iPhone developer? This chapter will show you how to create a very simple prototype level. Once you get into GameSalad you will truly enjoy it, the interface is so simple, and you never have to do any programming.

Many people dream of creating games, but unfortunately not many people possess the knowledge to find a suitable game engine (or create their own), to learn the language and start developing. Take for example, something as simple as moving your character around. When writing for the iPhone using Xcode, you would write something similar to the following:

```
-(void)walk_left {
  character.center = CGPointMake (character.center.x - 10,
  character.center.y);
}
```

That is just for moving the character, then you have to set up timers for the game, and an `NSMutableArray` for the character animation. Even when this is done, merely moving the character to the left with an animation will require more than 10 lines of code. Very few people have the time, or the patience to deal with coding (and of course the bugs). Thankfully, GameSalad has removed all these headaches; they have removed all coding, which means there's no chance of mistyping code, or forgetting a semicolon. If you do mistype something within the behaviors, it simply won't work, instead of throwing up a `SIGABRT` error or something nobody can understand. In order to make your character move, there is one simple drag-and-drop behavior. You are going to love GameSalad for its simplicity and power of use.

So, here is what we will discuss in this chapter. We are going to start slow and then we will get into the meatier stuff.

+ System requirements for developing
+ Registering with GameSalad and downloading it
+ Tour through GameSalad's user interface
+ How to create a GameSalad project
+ How to add moveable characters, platform collisions, win and death points
+ Add controls to your characters
+ Preview your game on your computer

Let's get to it shall we?

System requirements

In order for you to run GameSalad and create amazingly awesome games, you must meet the minimum system requirements, which are as follows:

+ Intel Mac (Any Mac from 2006 and above)
+ Mac OS X 10.6 or higher
+ At least 1GB RAM
+ A device running iOS (iPad, iPhone 3G and up, or iPod Touch)

If your computer exceeds these requirements, perfect! If not, you will need to upgrade your computer. Keep in mind, these are the **minimum** requirements; having a computer with better specs is recommended.

Let's get into GameSalad

Let's start by downloading GameSalad and registering for an account. Go to GameSalad's website, www.gamesalad.com and click the **Download Free App – GameSalad Creator** button.

While you are waiting for GameSalad to download, you should sign up for a free account. At the top of the page click **Sign Up**, enter your email address and create a username and password.

You have two options for GameSalad membership. You can keep the **Basic Pricing**, which is completely free or select **Professional Pricing**. The difference is when you publish your app, you will have a **Created with GameSalad** splash screen, not a big deal right? Especially not when you can get this awesome program for free! The professional pricing, which is $499 (USD) per year gives you all the features of the free version of GameSalad, plus it allows you to use iAds, Game Center, promotional links, your own custom splash screen, and priority technical support.

 This does not include your Apple developer cost, which is $99 a year.

Other tools that are recommended for game development:

◆ Adobe Photoshop (`http://www.adobe.com/products/photoshop.html`) or a free equivalent such as Inkscape, Gimp, or Pixelmator

◆ Drawing tablet (makes creating sprites much easier but not required)

Getting familiar with GameSalad's interface

Once you open GameSalad, you are presented with several options on screen.

Here they are in detail:

- **Home**: Shows you the latest GameSalad links (success stories, their latest game release, and so on...).

- **News**: This self-explanatory section shows you the latest update notes, and what is new in the GameSalad community.

- **Start**: The getting started screen, featuring video tutorials, wiki docs, blog, and more.

- **Profile**: This shows you, your GameSalad profile page, messages, followers, and likes.

- **New**: These are all your new projects, blank templates, and various barebone templates to get you started.

- **Recent**: This shows you all of your recently saved projects.

- **Portfolio**: This shows all your published Apps through GameSalad.

For now, let's click **New | My Great Project**

This is a fresh project; everything is empty. You can see that you have one level so far, but you can add more later on. See the Scenes and Actors tabs? Currently, **scenes** is selected showing you all of your levels, but if you click the **Actors** tab, you will be able to see all your actors (that is, game objects, characters, collectables, and so on). You can also label your actors with **tags**, to give you an idea of what these are useful for. If, for example you have 30 different enemies, when you are setting up your collisions within behaviors, you won't have to set up 30 different collisions. Rather, when you associate the relevant actors with a tag named Enemies, you can do a single collision behavior for all actors of the tag! This saves a lot of time when coding. We will get into more detail about actor tags, when we get into creating some games later in the book.

If you double-click on the **Initial Scene**, you will be taken to the level editor. Before we do that, let's go through the buttons shown in the following screenshot:

- **Back/Forward** buttons: Used when navigating back and forth between windows

- **Web Preview**: Allows you to see what your game will look like within the browser (HTML5)

- **Home**: This takes you right back to the project's main window

- **Publish**: Brings up the **Publish** window; here you can chose to deploy your game to the web, iPhone, iPad, Mac, or Android

- **Scenes**: Gives you a drop-down menu of all your scenes

- **Feedback**: Have some thoughts about GameSalad? Click this to send them to the creators!

- **Preview**: At the main menu, or while editing an actor, this starts your game from the beginning; if you are in a level, it will preview the level

- **Help**: Brings up the GameSalad documentation, which lists many help topics

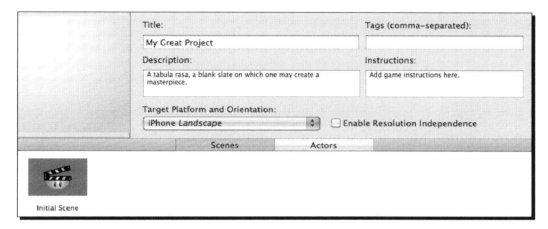

The descriptions of the buttons in the previous screenshot are as as follows:

- **Target Platform and Orientation**: This drop-down menu gives you, your device options: iPhone Landscape, iPhone Portrait, GameSalad.com, iPad Landscape, iPad Portrait, and 720p HD

- **Enable Resolution Independence** (only when iPhone and iPad device is set): Check this option if you are creating a game specifically for the iPhone 4, 4S, iPad, or Kindles and Nooks. This takes your high resolution images and converts them for iPhone 3GS, 3G, and iPhone (1st Gen)

- **Scenes** tab: Switch to this to see all your wonderful levels!

- **Actors** tab: Select this tab to see all the actors in your game project. From this tab, you can group different types of actors, such as platforms and enemies. This comes in handy when an actor has to collide with numerous other actors (enemies or platforms)

- + button: Adds a Level

- - button (when a level is selected): Deletes a level

Seems pretty easy, right? It is! GameSalad's user interface is simple. Even if you don't know what a certain button does, just hover your mouse over the button and a tooltip appears and tells you. Even though it's a very simple user interface, however, it is very powerful. Take for example, the **Enable Resolution Independence** option. Simply selecting this saves a lot of time from having to create two sets of images, a high resolution retina-friendly image, and a lower quality set for non-retina display images. With this option, all you have to do is create a high resolution set. GameSalad automatically creates a lower quality set of images for non-retina devices. How great is that? Such a simple option and yet it saves so much time and effort, and isn't simplicity what everyone wants?

Getting into the Scene Editor

Double-click the initial scene and you will see the **Scene Editor**, which may be a little daunting, but once you get used to the user interface it is really quite simple.

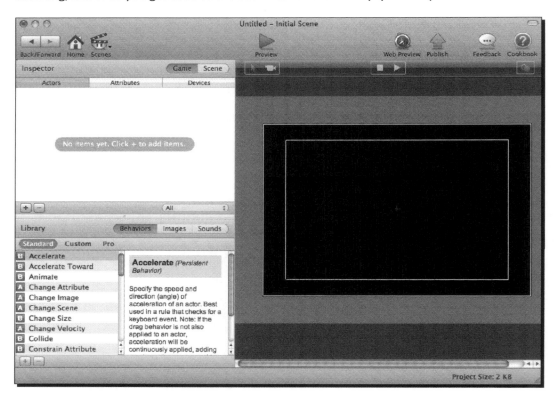

What do all these buttons mean? Following is a description of all the buttons and boxes:

◆ **Inspector** (with **Game** selected)

    ❑ **Actors**: All our in-game items (players, platforms, collectables, and so on).

    ❑ **Attributes**: Edit all the game attributes such as the display size.

    ❑ **Devices**: Edit all the settings for the mouse, touch screen, accelerometer, screen, and audio.

◆ **Inspector** (with **Scene** selected)

    ❑ **Attributes**: Edit all the attributes of the current level, such as the size of the level, screen wrap (X,Y), gravity, background color, camera settings, and autorotate.

    ❑ **Layers**: Create numerous layers and mark them as scrollable or not scrollable. For example, a layer called UI with scrollable deselected will have all your user interface items, and they could hold on the screen.

◆ **Library** (with **Behaviors** selected)

    ❑ **Standard**: All the standard GameSalad behaviors (movement, changing actor attributes, and more).

    ❑ **Custom**: Your own custom behaviors. Let's say you needed the same behavior for numerous actors but you didn't want to keep re-adding and changing the behavior for each actor. Once you create the behavior, drag it into this box and you can use it as much as you want.

    ❑ **Pro**: These are all the professional behaviors (only available when you have paid for the professional membership). These include Game Center Connect, iAd, and Open URL.

◆ **Library** (with **Images** selected)

    ❑ **Project**: This shows all the images imported into this project.

    ❑ **Purchased**: A new feature that shows the images you have purchased through GameSalad's Marketplace. (When you click **Purchase Images...**, this will take you to the GameSalad Marketplace where you will see a plethora of Content packs and more to purchase and import into your game).

    ❑ When you click the "+" button, you can import images from your hard drive; alternately, you can drag them directly into the **Library** from the **Finder.**

◆ **Library** (with **Sounds** selected)

Shows all the sound effects and music that you have imported into your project. As with images, when you click the "+" button you can import sound effects or music from your hard drive, or drag them directly in from the **Finder.**

- **Actor Mode**: This involves normal mouse functions; allows you to select actors within the level. Following is the screenshot of the icon:

- **Camera Mode**: Allows you to edit the camera, position, and scrolling hot spots for characters that control the camera. Following is the screenshot of the icon:

- **Reset Scene**: If this button is pressed while previewing your level, everything will go back to its initial state. Following is the screenshot of the icon:

- **Play**: This will start a preview of the current level (As distinct from the green **Project Preview** button, which previews the whole project). When you complete the level, an alert will appear telling you the scene has ended, and you can either select to preview the next level, or reset the current scene. Following is the screenshot of the icon:

- **Show Initial State**: If you are running a preview, and want to see the initial state without ending the preview, then pause, click on this icon and the initial state is seen. Following is the screenshot of the icon:

There we go! The GameSalad interface really is that easy to navigate! In this section, you set up an account with GameSalad, you downloaded and installed it and now you know how to use the interface. GameSalad has such a simple interface, but it is really powerful. As we saw earlier, an option as simple as Resolution Independence is so easy to select, and yet one click takes off so much time from creating different sets of images that can be used for developing. This is what makes GameSalad so great; it's such a simple user interface and yet it is so powerful. What is so amazing about all of it, is that there's no programming involved whatsoever! For those who don't have the coding skills to program a full game, this is just what they want; simple, quick, and super powerful.

Creating a new project!

Easy! Simply open up GameSalad and you meet the welcome screen. You will see on the sidebar that New is selected, so let's go ahead and open up the project **My Great Project**. Now, you have a blank slate to work with. Next, let's open up the level **Initial Scene**, which opens up the scene editor. Does it seem a little confusing? If so, don't worry, the user interface is so simple that you will be navigating around it in no time. What we are going to do in this chapter is make a simple (and I mean very simple) platform game.

Time for action – setting up a platform level

Okay, let's populate this level.

1. In the **Inspector** box, click on the + button, and you will see a new actor appear.

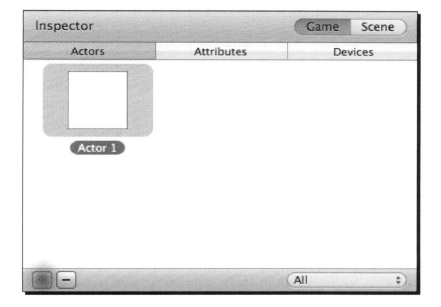

2. Next, double-click **Actor 1** and the actor editor will appear. Under the **Size** drop-down, change both **X** and **Y** to 32 for a smaller character. Have a look around the editor; we will spend a lot of time here. When you're done, click the **Back** button at the top to return to the scene editor.

3. Drag the actor into the level, press the **Play** button. Nothing happened? That is because we haven't added any gravity yet!

4. Under the **Inspector**, click **Scene | Gravity | Y** then add 300, or whatever you like; it all depends on what kind of level you are making, but I find 300 is a good gravity for regular levels. If you are creating a space level, make that number smaller for less gravity, if you are creating an underwater level, make it a larger number for more.

5. Now, press the **Play** button. Your character falls right off the screen. No worries, we just have to add a platform for your character to land on.

6. Under the **Inspector**, click **Game | +**, now you will have another actor named **Actor 2**. Let's make things a little easier here, double-click the name of the actor to rename it. For **Actor 1** change the name to Player and the name of **Actor 2** to Platform. Now double-click on **Platform**.

7. Go to the **Attributes**, and under **Size**, change **Width** to 350, and the **Height** to 10. Change the color to anything you like. Scroll down to **Physic** and change **Restitution** to 0. If you leave it at 1, it will make this platform bouncy, and right now we don't want that. Finally, uncheck the **Movable** box to prevent the platform from moving, again another thing we don't want.

8. Go back to the level editor. Drag the **Platform** actor into the level and place it underneath your actor. Press the **Play** button. The character falls as before, and the platform stays in place but the actor keeps falling and doesn't stop at the platform.

9. Double-click the **Player** actor. Under the **Attributes** box, scroll down and change the **Restitution** to 0 as we did for the Platform. Now in the Library, scroll through the **Behaviors** and find the **Collide** behavior. Drag it into the white box where it says **Drag your behaviors here**.

10. Change the drop-down box that says **Player** to **Platform**. Go back to the scene editor and press the **Play** button. The player falls and stops on the platform. If it doesn't, double-check you followed all the steps properly; usually, it can be the simplest thing you missed. That's OK! Things are looking pretty good, but now we are going to add some controls.

11. Double-click your **Player** actor to bring up the editor.

What just happened?

What did we just do here? We created a new actor and added some attributes to it to make it act like a platform. We also added gravity to the scene to make our actor move. Pretty simple isn't it? Especially when you compare GameSalad's collision detection to coding it:

```
CGRect rectOne =[charshot frame];
CGRect rectTwo =[target frame];
float leftMostOne = CGRectGetMinX(rectOne);
float leftMostTwo = CGRectGetMinX(rectTwo);
float rightMostOne = CGRectGetMaxX(rectOne);
float rightMostTwo = CGRectGetMaxX(rectTwo);
float topMostOne = CGRectGetMinY(rectOne);
float topMostTwo = CGRectGetMinY(rectTwo);
float bottomMostOne = CGRectGetMaxY(rectOne);
float bottomMostTwo = CGRectGetMaxY(rectTwo);
if((topMostOne < bottomMostTwo && bottomMostOne > topMostTwo) &&
  (leftMostOne < rightMostTwo && rightMostOne > leftMostTwo)) {
  gameState = kGameStatePaused; // Pause the game
  UIAlertView *alert = [[UIAlertView alloc]
    //Bring up text saying nice shot
  initWithTitle:nil
  message:@"Nice Shot!"
  delegate:self
  cancelButtonTitle:nil
  otherButtonTitles:@"Continue", nil];
  [alert show];
  [alert release];
  target.center = CGPointMake(target.center.x, enemyY);
    //change to random position
  charShot.center = CGPointMake(0, 0);
    //Change character shot to x-0 y-0
  shooting = NO;
    //turns off a boolean so the character stops shooting
  immunity.progress = immunity.progress + .10; //add to score
}
```

Yes, I don't think too many people want to do that... Let's keep going!

Have a go hero

We created a normal platform movement, but try doing this:

- Create a space scene (lower gravity)
- Create different platform types such as super bouncy or sticky

Play around with the settings and you'll be going in no time!

Time for action – let's make your player move!

In this section, we are going to start adding some movement for our character. We will add simple left and right motions. We won't deal with jumping just yet though.

1. Click on **Create Group**, rename the group to Controls.

2. Click on **Create Rule** and drag the rule into your **Controls** group, just to keep things organized. When you start adding more behaviors, it can get pretty cluttered. Rename the rule to Move Left, then click the middle drop-down box and change it from **mouse button** to **key**.

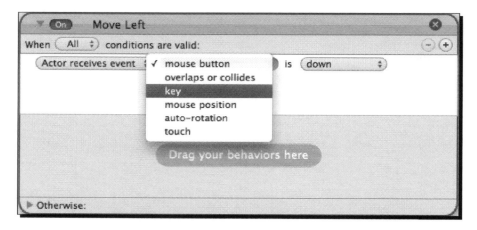

3. Click the **Keyboard** button and an image of a keyboard will pop up. Now, click the left arrow key on the keyboard.

4. Go to the **Library** and find the **Move** behavior and drag it into the rule (be sure you drag it into the rule, if you don't, the player will keep moving whether a key is pressed or not.)

5. Change the **Behavior** settings in the previous screenshot, **Direction** – 180, **Speed** – 100, and everything else can be left as it is.

6. Repeat the above steps to create a second <bold> Move behavior within **Controls**, this time for right movement with the Right arrow key.. You can easily duplicate a behavior/rule by selecting *Option* and clicking-and-dragging the new duplicate to anywhere you like.

7. Go back to the scene editor and test it out. Now, you'll be able to move back and forth across the platform. This is kind of boring though, isn't it? Let's add a level end, and a death point.

What just happened?

We added some life to our actor by adding a couple of super simple behaviors and rules. He can now move left and right, he is affected by gravity, and he can collide with other actors.

Now, we are going to add the ending points for our level, a death and a win point.

Have a go hero

Play around with some of the movements, try doing a mouse movement, or if you're feeling adventurous, try doing some touch or accelerometer motion.

Time for action – create ways to win or lose

Your level needs something more... all you can do is move around, don't you think we should finish it? Let's add a door for your character to enter and win the level, and let's make your actor die when he falls off the platform. First, we are going to create a way for the player to win:

1. Go back to the level editor and use **Inspector** to create another actor. Click on **Actor 3**, change its **Width** to 32, **Height** to 50, **Color** to gold (or whatever you like), uncheck **movable**, and rename it to Door. Everything else can be left as it is.

2. Back in the level editor, drag the door into the level at a place where your player will be able to reach it. Double-click your actor in the **Inspector**, not in the level. If you edit the one in the level, you are editing a copy of the original and any changes you make will not be reflected on the actor in the **Inspector**. This can be good if you need to make per-level changes, but normally you would edit the original actor to make universal changes. Next create another rule and call it **Level Win**. Change the middle drop-down box from **mouse button** to **overlaps or collides**, and change the last drop-down box (the one that says **Player**) to **Door**.

3. In the **Library**, scroll down to find the **Display Text** behavior, drag it into the **Level Win** rule. Change the text to You Win!

4. Add a **Timer** behavior. Change the drop-down box that says **Every** to **After** and the time from 5 to 1.

5. Find the **Reset Scene** behavior and drag it into the timer.

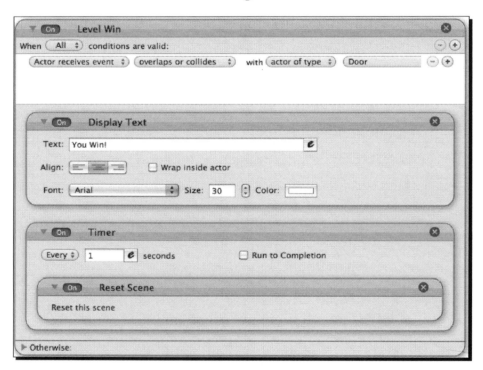

6. Test it. When your player touches the door **You Win!** appears on your character. After one second it will reset the scene.

Pretty beautiful isn't it? It reminds me of the old Atari games I used to play when I was a kid. We can do better!

7. Let's go and add the **Kill zone**, or an actor that will kill your **Player** actor on contact. In the level editor, under the **Inspector** create another actor (don't forget you press the + button to create actors!). Rename it to Kill Zone.

8. Double-click **Kill Zone**, change the **width** to 480 (the full width of the iPhone screen), and turn off **movable**.

9. Go back to the level editor and drag the **Kill zone** actor to the level, just underneath the platform.

10. Double-click the **Player** actor, create a new rule, and rename it to Player Death or something delightfully horrible like that.

11. Just as with our door, change the middle drop-down box from **mouse button** to **overlaps or collides**, and change the last drop-down box from **Player** to **Kill Zone**.

12. In the **Behavior** section, find the **Reset Scene** behavior and drag it into the rule.

13. Looks good right? That's it! Still, that **Kill zone** is a sore sight, let's hide it. Double-click the **Kill Zone** actor, and under **Graphics** uncheck **Visible**.

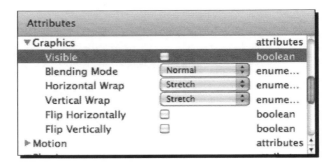

And that's everything! Seems pretty easy right? It totally is! Let's see our finished project:

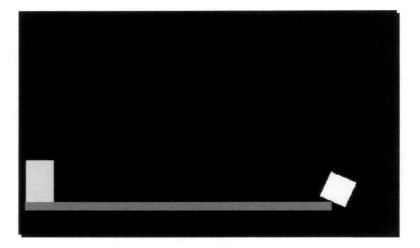

Uh oh... I know what's going to happen next! Do you want to preview your game?

Simply click the green arrow at the top of GameSalad's interface! You will get an exact preview of what your game will look like.

That is all that's involved in prototyping your game! Need a quick idea of what your game is going to do? Want to see how it will look or play out before you have everything ready to develop? Do what we did in this chapter, you don't need all the fancy images, you just need to see how things will feel and perform on the target devices. In this chapter, you were able to create a new GameSalad project, get familiar with some simple behaviors, keyboard controls, and collisions, and you learned how to preview your game without deploying it to a device. Quiz time!

Pop quiz

1. What is the minimum amount of RAM required to run GameSalad?

    a. 256MB

    b. 1GB

    c. 2GB

    d. 4GB

2. How do you create a new project in GameSalad?

    a. **File | New...**

    b. *command* key + *N*

    c. Click **New** on the side bar, and select the blank template you want

    d. *Control + N*

3. How do you change the gravity in a scene?

    a. **Edit | Gravity** and change the slider to the desired amount

    b. **Inspector | Scene |** change the X and Y values

    c. *command* key + *G*

    d. *Shift + G*

Summary

In this chapter, we had a small tour through GameSalad's interface, learned how to create a new project, and we even made our own prototype game! Using GameSalad, you got an idea of how simple it is, how one simple collide behavior can save so much time compared to coding it. Imagine 27 lines of code to do something that requires just 5 behaviors in GameSalad. Now that you see how simple GameSalad is, are you not happy you are using it? The frustrations of coding are not something everyone wants to put up with, especially not when there's a tool as simple as GameSalad out there!

3
Add Zest to your Salad

Mmm... zesty salad! Don't you prefer a salad that has some kind of dressing on it as opposed to just lettuce? Yeah, me too. It adds a kick to a normally plain food. Essentially, that is what we are going to do in our game; we are going to add a zesty dressing, mmm... yummy!

In the previous chapter, we created a prototype game - nothing special, just a quick little "engine test" you could say. In this chapter, we are going to add magic to that prototype. We will learn to design some sprites in Photoshop and even some 3D sprite tips for better looking graphics. We are then going to import our images, some music, and sound effects into our game. We will trigger audio in the level, and add some cool particle effects, all to make our game look even better! We are going to be looking at some very important stuff here; the better your graphics, music, and sound effects are, the more appealing your game will be. When someone sees some really cool or realistic graphics, they will be more inclined to purchase your game, as opposed to some ugly looking graphics that are complete eyesores, then no one will want to buy it, or if they do, it's just because it's so horrible.

Let's take a look at what we are going to cover in this chapter:

◆ Tips on designing sprites

◆ Importing your images, sound effects, and music into your game

◆ Triggering music and sound effects in your game

◆ Working with particles

Sounds exciting, doesn't it? Well then, what are we waiting for? Let's get into it!

Designing sprites

As mentioned in the introduction of this chapter, images or sprites are very important for your game. There are a plethora of tools available for sprite design; my favorites are Adobe Photoshop CS5 and Adobe Flash CS5. Both do different image styles; Flash, in my opinion, gives a great hand-drawn look to the images you create.

An image with a nice hand-drawn look, created with Adobe Flash is as follows:

I think that it looks fantastic, not exactly the image itself but the style of the brush, it's nice and smooth, and everything seems to flow together and looks great. Now, let's take a look at an image drawn with Photoshop.

With Photoshop, the edges are sharp and everything looks crisp. Whichever art style you prefer is up to you; each of these programs have their advantage, but what if you cannot afford them? After all, Photoshop and Flash are worth over $600 each. Well, there are many free tools out there, Gimp, Inkscape, or even MS Paint if you have access to it, and they can draw sprites just as well as Photoshop.

Usually, sprites are put onto a sprite sheet, which is exactly what it sounds like, a page of sprites. These are useful when creating a game with Xcode, OpenGL ES, or Cocos2D. These engines allow you to import a single sprite sheet and display different sections of the sheet programmatically. GameSalad eliminates the need for this, however, so we are going to be creating single images instead of a whole sheet.

Sprites are normally 32x32 pixels, and are saved as a PNG (Portable Network Graphics) image. PNGs are the best for quality, plus they have an **alpha channel** for transparency, so when you import your image into GameSalad, there isn't a white background surrounding your sprite.

In the following screenshot, the image with the white background is a JPEG and the image with no white background is saved as a PNG:

If you have a drawing tablet, grab it now. If you don't have one, it's a great idea to get one, it's way more accurate and if you draw well you can skillfully create your images with no problem. If you don't want one, that's ok too because you can use a lot of shapes to create your character, which is what we are going to do in this chapter. We are going to create a character for the game we created in our last chapter. Then we will import it into our game, along with an image for our platforms. I'm going to be using Photoshop, but again, you can use whatever tool you like.

Time for action – let's create our character!

For this section, we are going to take a look at creating a character (or sprite) within Photoshop, but you can use what you learn in any of your favorite imaging programs.

1. Open up Photoshop, and click **File | New** or **command + N**, change the **Width** and **Height** to 32, and make sure under **Background Contents** we select Transparent. Be sure the **Resolution** is 72 not 72.0009, as this can cause image quality issues.

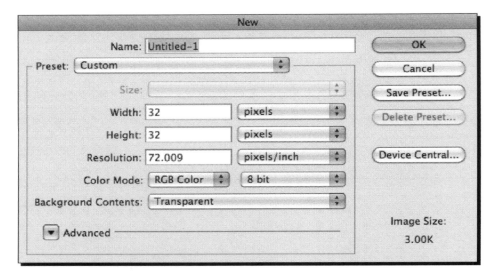

2. Find the **Rectangle Tool**, click and hold until the menu pops up, and click the **Custom Shape Tool**.

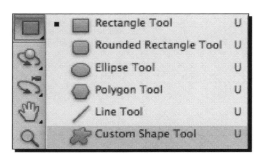

3. Let's create the outline of our character, we are going to draw a box around the outline of the canvas.On the tool bar at the top, click the **Shape** drop-down menu, scroll down and find the **Square Thin** Frame, If you cannot find this menu, click the circle with the black triangle in it, and the preset menu will appear. Now click **Shapes** to find it.

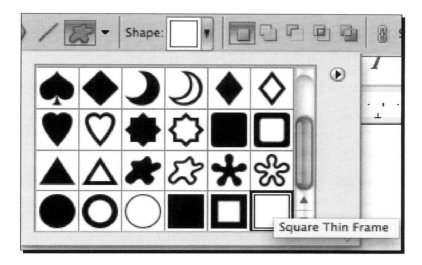

4. Click-and-drag a shape with the same size as the canvas. Then click the **Paint Bucket Tool**, chose a color you like and fill in the box you just created. When you click to fill in the box, you will get a pop-up saying "**This shape layer must be rasterized before proceeding. It will no longer have a vector mask. Rasterize the shape?**" Click **OK**.

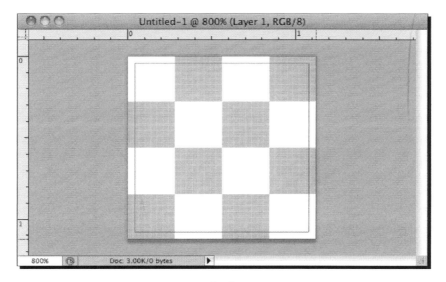

5. As you can see there is some transparency shown, so press *command + J* twice. This will duplicate the layer 2 times, thus filling in the transparent edges.

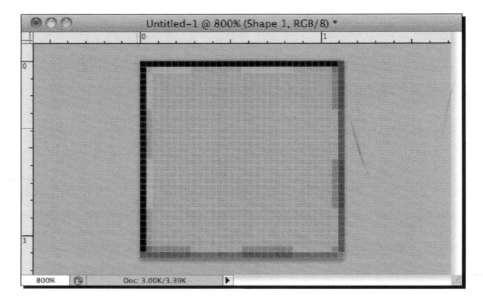

6. Let's draw in some eyes, and a mouth to add some character to your... well, your character. Use the Pencil tool as shown in the following figure to draw in some eyes, pupils and a mouth.

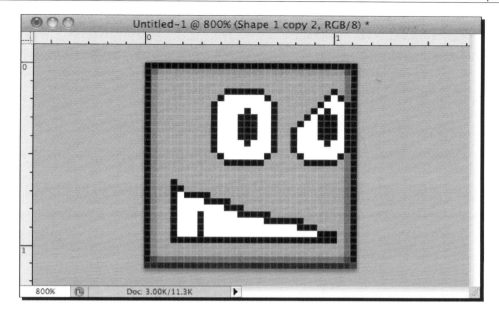

7. That's it! Or is it? The character looks a little.... oh I don't know, dull?! Let's add some shading. (Don't forget you can press *I* to use the **Eye Drop Tool** too, to pick a color, then you can choose a darker version of it in the color picker.)

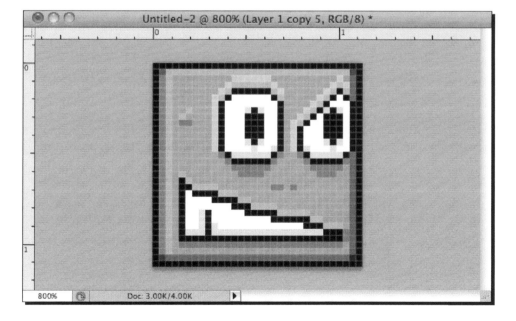

8. Let's just add one more final touch to our character. Click on **Filter | Texture | Texturizer**. Use any settings you like, I used **Canvas**, 50% **Scaling** and 2 **Relief**.

9. You can use any of the textures that you want, there is **Brick**, **Burlap**, **Canvas**, or **Sandstone**. Play around with the options and select whatever you like.

10. Let's import it into GameSalad! Save your image as a PNG, and open the project you created in the previous chapter. Open up the **Initial Scene | Library | Images | +** button, and browse and import your character. Your image will now appear in your image **Library**.

11. Now simply click-and-drag the image onto your character and that's it! Well, not quite; next we are going to create an image for your platform.

What just happened?

In this section, we learned how to create a simple, yet cool-looking sprite. We looked at drawing simple shapes, and then we added some shading, and highlights to give the image more depth and realism to make it look more appealing.

Have a go hero

Try designing your own character. Make him look as cartoony or cool as you like. If you don't need any transparency, you may save it as a JPEG, but if you do have see-through bits then you have to save it as a PNG, because this file type includes an alpha (transparency) channel.

Time for action – let's draw a platform

Okay, now that we have our player looking awesome, why don't we make the rest of the level look good? Let's start by making our platform look cool.

1. Open up Photoshop, or whatever you are using. Don't forget, for our platform we set the size as **Width** to 350 and **Height** to 10, so when you create the new image, set the **Canvas** size accordingly.

2. Click the **Paint Bucket Tool**, click your favorite color and fill in the **Canvas**. Click **Filter | Texture | Patchwork** and change the **Square Size** to 10, and the **Relief** to 25.

3. As before, import it into GameSalad. Save your image as a PNG, and open the project you created in our last chapter. Open up the **Initial Scene | Library | Images | +** button, and browse and import your character. Your image will now appear in **Image | Library**.

4. Drag the image from the **Library** onto your character in the **Inspector**. Something isn't quite right, why is your platform not the same color as your image? Double-click your **Platform** actor, and change the color to white.

What just happened?

In this section, we added some more flair to our level by creating a good-looking image for our platform. This simple step makes the whole level look much better.

Have a go hero

Design your own image for the platform; add any texture you like or any effect to make it look cool!

Time for action – let's draw our door

As with our last section, we will make our level look a little better by creating an image for our door.

1. Create another image for the door. This can be a wooden door, a metal door, or you can even create a door image as in Super Mario Bros. 2.—just a simple white glowing box. Remember the **Width** was 32 and the **Height** was 50. Import it into GameSalad and drag the image on to the door actor. Looks better, doesn't it?

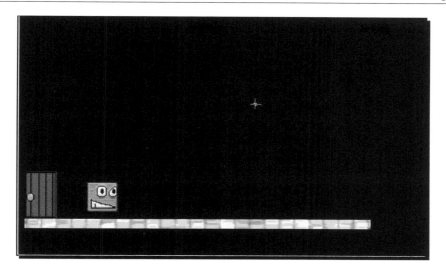

2. Let's actually make the level bigger now. In the **Inspector | Scene | Size** drop-down, change the **Width** to 1500. As you can see, you now have a larger level to work with, so click-and-drag a bunch of Platforms actors in any arrangement you like, rotate them, it's your level! Here is mine, nothing amazing for now.

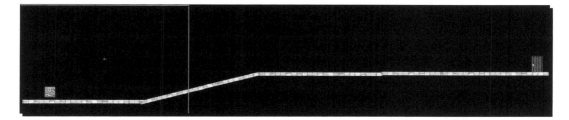

3. Click the **Camera Mode** button. Drag the hot spot zones to match the next image.

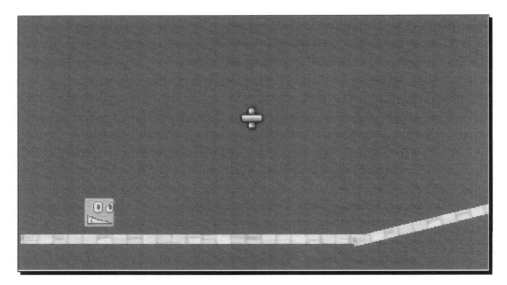

4. The hot spot zones have been changed, so when the actor reaches the center of the screen, the camera will follow. Speaking of cameras we need to add the behavior to scroll the camera. Double-click our **character** actor, find the **Control Camera** behavior, drag it into your actor's behaviors and that's it! Your player will now control the movement of the camera.

What just happened?

In this section, we made our level look better by creating and importing an image for our door into the game. We also arranged multiple actors within GameSalad to create a level, and we set the scene up for our character to control the camera.

Have a go hero

Design your own level; create multiple platforms for your characters to walk on to reach the end of the level. Have them moving up and down, rotated or flat. Whatever you like, give it a try!

Time for action – Let's add some sound

What game would be complete without sounds? None! Could you imagine playing Uncharted with no voice overs, or the incredible soundtrack? Or Portal without the witty dialogue of GlaDOS? Even the small sounds that you hear - a bird chirping in the background of an immense mountain range, or objects flying by you as they emerge from an explosion - without all these effects, games just wouldn't be complete, would they? So, let's add some to ours!

1. We are going to add some music and a dying sound effect into our level. Search for a sound effect and a song you like; GameSalad reads a bunch of formats including MP3 and WAV and then it converts them to OGG. This is great considering that earlier versions didn't read any other format, you had to import OGG files. Import your sounds the same way you imported your images (click the + button, or drag them in from **Finder**), in the **Library** select **Sounds** instead of **Images**. You will be asked if you want to import the file as a sound effect or music; select accordingly.

2. Let's trigger both of these. One will be for the background music, and the other will be the death sound effect. Double-click your **Player** actor, expand the **Player Death** group, and add the **Play Sound** behavior.

To save yourself the time of dragging in this actor and scrolling through a list of sounds, you can drag the sound effect directly into the open actor. Doing this, will create the **Play Sound** behavior with the sound effect selected. Easy huh?

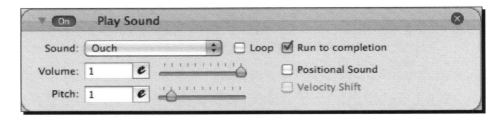

3. Select your sound effect from the list. You can tweak the settings to your liking, volume, pitch, and so on... The **Positional Sound** setting is great if you want a sound to get louder as you approach it, such as torches or gunfire.

4. We can do the same for music; drag in a **Play Music** behavior wherever you like (but not into a rule - we want the music to start right away and not have to be triggered) and select your music file, which you can choose whether to loop or not.

5. You can now test your level and see how everything plays out. If you followed everything correctly, you will now hear music and also a sound when you die. Your game is really coming together, but let's make it a little snazzy! Particle time!

What just happened?

In this section, we made our game much better by adding some sound effects, and as mentioned in the introduction of this section, what game would be complete without them?

Time for action – let's create some particles

1. Create a new actor in your **Inspector**, rename it to Torch, double-click it and let's make it burn baby! Change the size to 10x10, expand the **Color** settings, and change the **Alpha** to 0—this will make it invisible, and under **Physics** uncheck **Movable**.

2. Drag in a **Particles** behavior and change the settings to the following:

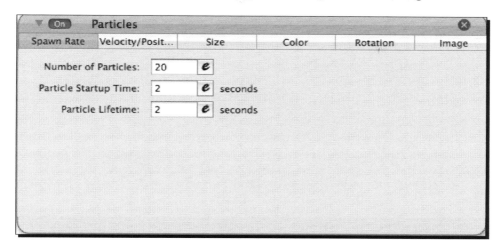

- ◆ **Spawn Rate** Tab
    - ❑ **Number Of Particles**: 100
    - ❑ **Particle Lifetime**: 4
- ◆ **Velocity/Position** Tab
    - ❑ **Direction**: 90
    - ❑ **Speed**: 20
- ◆ **Size** Tab
    - ❑ Change the **Size does not change** drop-down to **Size Changes to**
    - ❑ **Target Size**: 0
    - ❑ **Duration**: 2
- ◆ **Color** Tab
    - ❑ Change the "**Color does not change**" drop-down to "**Color changes to**"
    - ❑ **Target Color**: Black
    - ❑ **Duration**: 2
- ◆ **Rotation** Tab
    - ❑ **Angular Velocity**: 20

Again, these are just suggestions, you can change them to whatever you like you can add a little flame like I did, or you can do a full-on blaze! (Hint: You can also add another particle behavior for smoke. Add a longer lifetime, bigger target size, change the base color to gray, the target color to black, and you will have thick smoke.)

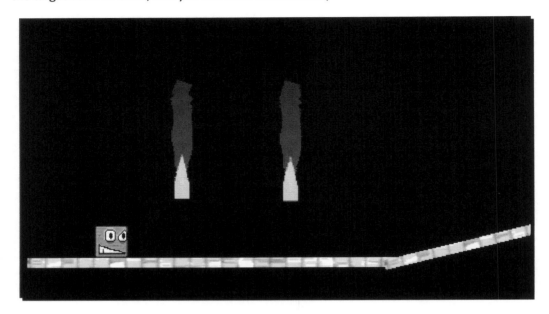

"Nice-looking torches with great-looking smoke."

What just happened?

In this section, we added some excellent-looking particle effects. Granted these are very simple but they still look awesome! Later in the book, we are going to make realistic particles, but let's take this one step at a time.

Have a go hero

Play around with some of the particle effects settings. Set them to your liking; the more you play with them, the more likely you are to find a style you like. You can add an image to the particles to make them look more realistic too.

Time for action – let's add some levels

1. Let's add some more to our little game. We are going to add a main menu, another level, and a **You win** screen.

2. Go to the **Home** screen of your GameSalad project. At the bottom click the **+** button to add a new level, this will be our menu. Click-and-drag the new level on the **Initial scene**, so that it is now our first level and rename it to Menu or whatever you like.

3. Open up your level, and arrange it any way you like. This is just something simple, so we aren't going crazy yet.

4. Create a new actor, name it Button. Open up the **Button** actor, and change the **Color | Alpha** to 0.

5. Add a **Display Text** behavior, and change the text to Start Game.

6. Create a new rule; change the middle drop-down box to **mouse button**.

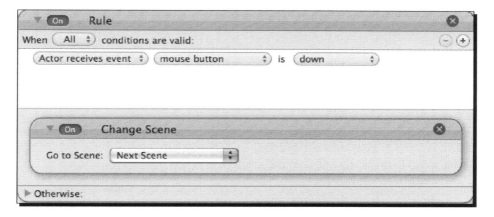

7. Add a **Change Scene** behavior to the rule, and make sure the **Go to Scene** drop-down menu has **Next Scene** selected.

8. Test your game and make sure when you click your button, it goes to the next level. If it doesn't, something hasn't gone right; go back and fix it!

9. Go back to the project home page and create a new level, change the name to Level 2.

10. Open up your new level, change the level size. This time, let's make it a high level, let's say, **Height** at 1500 and leave the **Width** at 480, and change the **Gravity** to 300.

11. Put your character at the top of the level, and create a platform under him/her.

12. Place a whole bunch of platforms lower and lower until you reach the bottom of the level.

13. Add a door at the bottom of the level so the player can win.

14. Let's not forget the **Kill zones**. Create 3 **Kill zones**, two on the side and stretch them to match the height of the level, and the one at the bottom.

15. Don't change the camera because, as it is, the player has to reach the bottom of the screen until the camera scrolls. This makes it more challenging for the player.

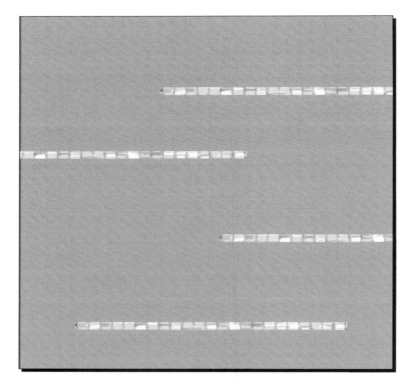

What just happened?

In this section, we added some more levels, a menu, plus another level with a different size and more platforms.

This is what I did, the player can't see below, so it's a guessing game as if they are going to hit a platform or fall to their death!

Time for action – winning the level

Let's finish the game by adding a simple **You Win** screen to reward the player for their hard work.

1. Create a new level, and rename it `Win`, `end`, `ta-da`, or `lalalala`, whatever you want to call it.

2. Open up your **Win** level, and drag your Button actor into the middle of the screen.

3. Double-click the Button actor in the level, not in the **Inspector**.

4. You will see the previous screen. Do what it says, **Click the lock to edit the behaviors of this actor**. You will be editing just this actor, not the original.

5. Change the text to `You Win!`

6. Change the **Change Scene** rule from **Next Scene** to **Menu**.

7. Play your game through, notice something that's not quite right? You win a level and it resets the current level. Let's fix that.

8. Double-click the character actor, and expand the **Level Win** group.

9. Delete the **Display Text** behavior, and the timer.

10. Add a **Change Scene** behavior into the **Level Win** rule.

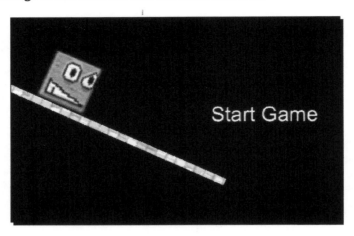

Our simple but lovely main menu

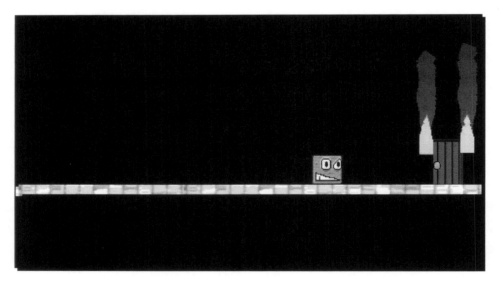

Our first level, yay! Our player made it!

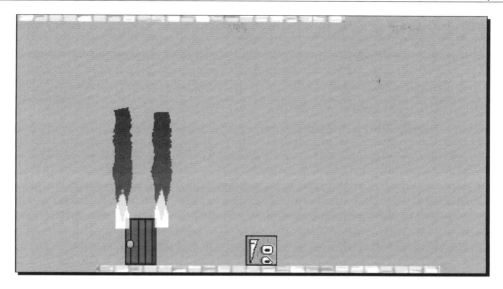

The second level, looks like our player had a bit of an accident, cool torches though!

And finally, our final level congratulating our player for winning.

That was all pretty easy, wasn't it? The game looks good with the sprites we drew, the sound effects make the game so much better, and the particles look fantastic. But what if you don't like the drawn 2D sprites for your character? That's quite alright, not all games look good with a cartoon style to them. Let's look at some 3D options. For this section, we are going to use 3D Studio Max 2010, in my opinion the easiest 3D modeling and animation program out there, but there are other options, Maya, Softimage XSi, or the way more cheap (free) Blender.

Using a 3D modeling tool is great for sprites because if you know how to texture and light the models properly, you can get a very realistic sprite, which is very appealing to the players. OK! Let's get into it.

Open up your modeling tool, and you may be a little lost by the interface but not to worry, they are really quite easy to navigate. We are going to create a simple character, just like the one we drew in Photoshop.

Time for action – let's make a better-looking character

This is the 3D Studio Max interface, it looks quite confusing, doesn't it? It's actually simple. I've used 3D Studio Max since I was in school and I love it. I made a couple of movies and animated into live-action video, anyways enough rambling.

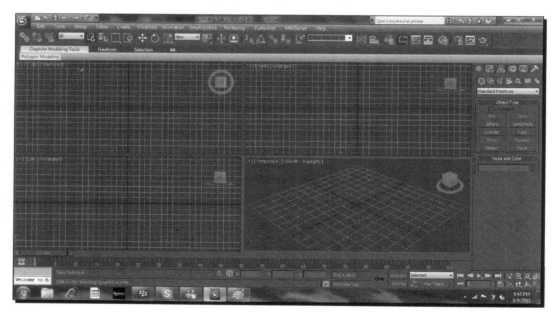

1. Let's get into some simple character creation! Let's start off by creating a box.

2. The dimensions of the box are 20x20x20, (that is, **Length**, **Width**, and **Height** are `20.0`)

3. Change the segments to `10` each, this will make it easier for editing the shape of the box later, The more segments you have, the more flexibility you will have when modeling. We are going to make the box rounder.

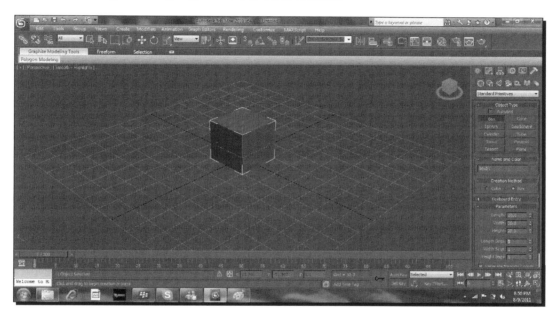

4. Next create a sphere, and stretch it along the Z axis (in layman's terms, "we are going to make it taller").

5. *Shift* + click the sphere to clone it, then scale it down to make the pupil of an eye.

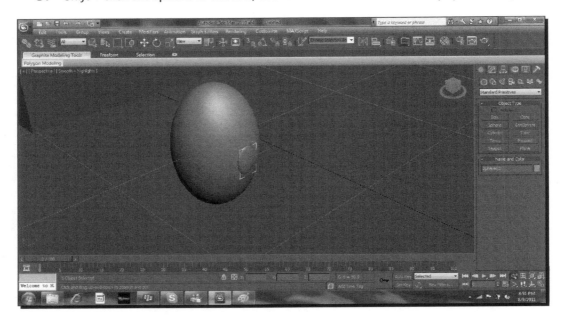

6. Now let's move the eye to the face, and clone the eye and pupil to make a 2nd eye.

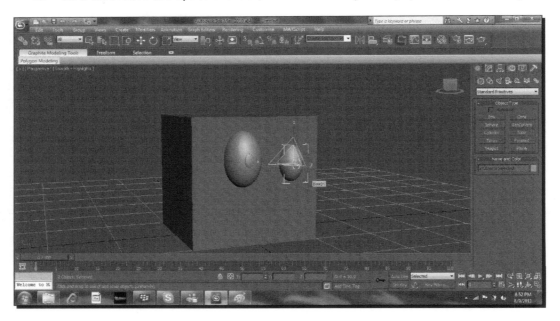

7. Create another sphere, but make it longer, and flatten it along the Y axis.

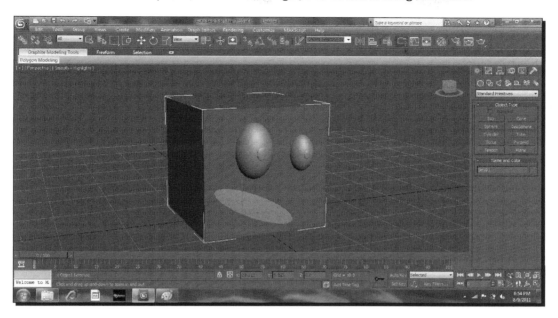

8. Drag the new sphere on the box for the mouth. Now, we are going to look after the textures.

9. Open up the **Material Editor**. I used the following settings:

- **Diffuse**: Orange
- **Specular Level**: around 170
- **Glossiness**: 28
- **Reflection | Falloff | Falloff Type | Fresnel** (For a reflection around the edges)
- **Bump | Speckle**: 2 strength

The given settings can be seen in action in the following screenshot.

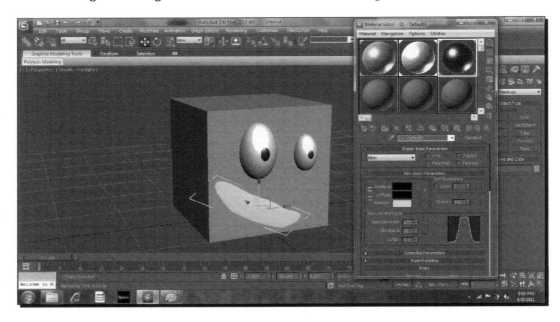

10. Drag the new material to the body of our character.

11. Duplicate the material twice and change the color of one to white and the other to black. Drag the whites to the eyes and the mouth, and the black to the pupils.

12. You could give the mouth more of a smile and reposition it to directly underneath the eyes. I have added a **Mesh Smooth** to the box to round out the edges.

13. Create an **omni light** and move it in front and off to the side of the character.

14. Press the *F* button to get to the **Front View**.

15. Now we are going to render the character. Press *F10* to bring up the render dialogue, and change the render size to 50x50.

16. Adjust the camera and light, so you can see the character at its best.

Now save this image as a `PNG` and let's move on to the platform image.

1. Create a long and thin box approximately 350x10 (there's no need to edit the segments on this box because we aren't going to be manipulating them).

2. Go to the **Material Editor**.

3. Change the material **Diffuse** to **Bitmap** and select a texture of your choice. Textures are so easy to find, simply search for something like "Wood Texture" and you'll be able to find one, no problem!

4. Remove the **Specular, Glossiness,** and **Reflection**.

5. Drag the **Map** from the **Diffuse** to the **Bump**, and change the strength from 2 to 100.

6. Render the image and save it as a PNG.

7. That's it! Let's import these new images into GameSalad and drag the new images into the **Character** and **Platform** actors.

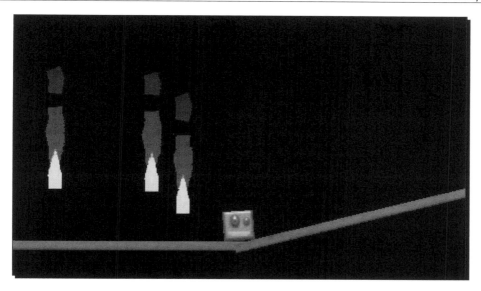

We have our new updated images in our first level, it looks beautiful! The torches look quite excellent too, don't they?

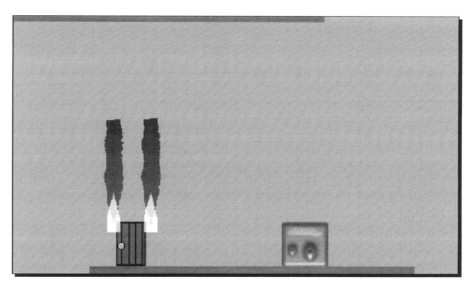

Looks like our player had another accident, but hey, the level looks good!

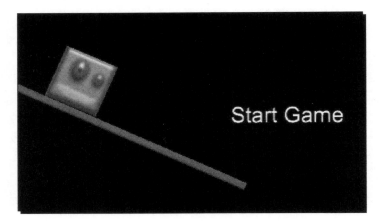

What just happened?

In this section, we looked at an alternate method for creating sprites, using 3D software. This comes in handy when you want to create a realistic-looking game, or it can even be used to create cartoony-looking games! It all depends on what your preference is.

Have a go hero

If you're able to, create a 3D character on your own, make him look awesome!

You can of course do more with 3D images, such as using it on the background and the door. Both the rendered images and the hand-drawn images have their advantages. You can draw cartoony and realistic images with both Photoshop and 3D Studio Max, you just need to know how to do it. With Photoshop you can use textures, lighting effects, and more, or you can keep it all solid colors and thick black outlines for the cartoon look. With 3D Studio Max, you can do realistic images with nice textures, reflections, glossiness, lighting, and bump maps for the realistic look, or you can use the **Ink and Paint** map for the cel-shaded cartoon look. This effect was made famous in The Legend of Zelda: Wind Waker. It all depends on which software you find it easier to use.

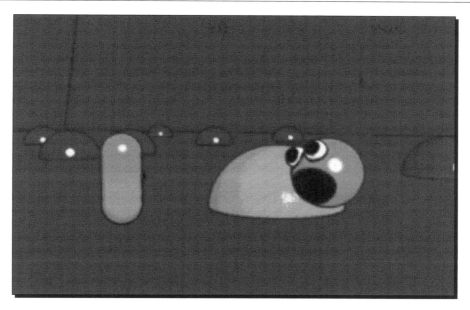

The previous screenshot is from the introduction video of iMMUNE, my first game released on the App Store. The whole game was created with 3D Studio Max **Ink and Paint** textures.

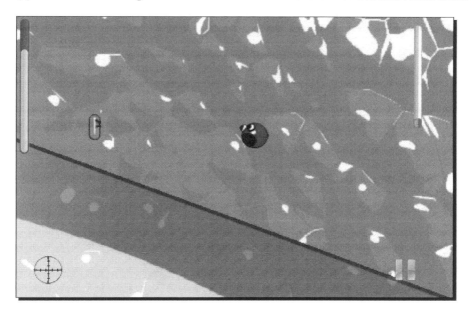

The previous screenshot is from iMMUNE, all the characters and background images were rendered with the **Ink and Paint** tool; as you can see, when put together they have a funky cartoon look to them that really looks nice. The next image was created with a mix of 3D Studio Max and Photoshop. When done right, they can both look either realistic or cartoon.

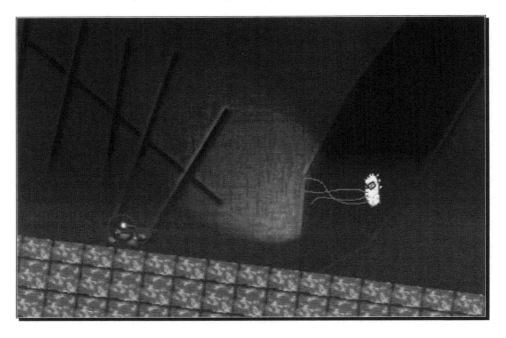

Are you getting all revved up to create a better game? Do you know what art style you want to use? Are you going for a hilarious action-comedy like Angry Birds? Or are you making a dark realistic game like Abuse? You may be able to start creating a game right now, but we haven't really dealt with any of the more complex areas of GameSalad, so just be patient, we are getting there. QUIZ TIME!

Pop quiz

1. What is the normal size for a sprite?

    a. 100x100

    b. 50x50

    c. 32x32

    d. 25x25

2. What is the best file type for sprites?

    a. JPEG

    b. GIF

    c. BMP

    d. PNG

3. What is the advantage of using PNG over other formats?

    a. Higher Quality, lower file size

    b. Transparency

    c. Flexible for editing

    d. All of the above

Summary

In this chapter, we learned some tips on how to create some sprites using Photoshop and to design good-looking 2D sprites, save them as a PNG and import them into GameSalad. We also learned how to import sound effects and music into our game and trigger them within the level. We got into GameSalad's particle effects a little bit, by creating some torches with a flame and some smoke. Finally, we looked at some other options on creating sprites, such as using 3D Studio Max to create a 3D version of our character, texture him, and render him with lighting. We also created a better-looking platform image. Then we imported them into GameSalad, and replaced our old images with the new ones.

As we continue through this book, you will begin to see how much time GameSalad saves you, and how much fun it can be to develop with it. We are going to learn a lot more in this book, so buckle your seat belts my friend, it's going to be a wild ride! In the next chapter, we are going to start a game entitled **Ball Drop**. The chapter is going to be divided into two parts, so you can breathe in between and reflect on what we've done.

Next, we are going to learn how to create a fully fledged game, complete with physics, a main menu (better than the one we just did), and touch controls.

By the end of this chapter, you will have the canvas of the game finished, and then we will start to add the behaviors.

4
Starting Simple: Ball Drop Part 1

Have you ever played The Incredible Machine? If you were going to school when this game first came out, like me, you most likely played it for hours and hours in the tech lab or library because you were completely addicted to it. We are going to make a game similar to it, a game where you have to get a ball into a basket by selecting and moving blocks around to reach the goal; the later levels will have obstacles that will destroy the ball. Plus to make it even more difficult, each level will have a timer, and if you don't solve it within the set amount of time, you will have to restart the level! How is that similar to The Incredible Machine? Well maybe it isn't but it's going to be a fun game.

We will code everything in the next chapter; first we will design all the levels. In this chapter, we will:

- ◆ Design the sprites for the game
- ◆ Design the levels within GameSalad

We are going to design the foundation of a game called **Ball Drop**. We are going to design the graphics, a few levels, and a menu system. We are going to start slow, but we have a lot to cover, so let's get to it shall we?

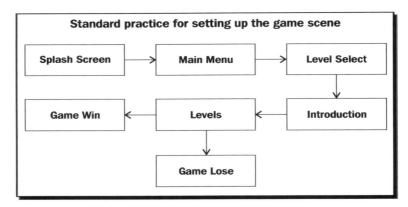

This figure shows how I go about designing and setting up my games, starting with the splash screen, on to the main menu ,and so on.

Let's create our sprites

The **Ball**, as shown in the following screenshot:

The **Platform**, as shown in the following screenshot:

The **Basket**, as shown in the following screenshot:

These are the sprites that we are going to be using in this project, but of course you can create your own sprites and make them look as cool as you like.

Have a go hero

Try designing your own sprites; whether you like the cartoony style, or the realistic look, it's up to you! Give it a go!

Time for action – let's get this project started

Ok let's go!

1. Open up **GameSalad**, click the **+ New** button, then click **My Great Project**, and just to make things a little more organized fill out all the project information.

2. Change the **Title** to "Ball Drop" or whatever you would like to call it, like "Super fun awesome bouncy game", and just to be safe let's uncheck **Enable Resolution Independence**. If you decide to publish your game to the App Store, then it will look great on all devices whether retina display or normal.

> **Tech tip**
>
> Graphics that you import should be two times (2x) the size that they appear in the scene, and with dimensions divisible by 4. The reason that most systems (even many modern graphics cards) demand power of two textures is **mipmapping**.
>
>
>
> In mipmapping, smaller versions of an image are created in order to make the image look proper at a very small size. The resolution is divided by 2 repeatedly to make new images.
>
> So, imagine a 256x128 image. This would have smaller versions created of dimensions 128x64, 64x32, 32x16, 16x8, 8x4, 4x2, 2x1, and 1x1.
>
> If this image was 256x192, it would work fine until you got down to a size of 4x3. The next smaller image would be 2x1.5, which is obviously not a valid size. Some graphics hardware can deal with this, but many types cannot.

3. Now we are going to create the **MAIN MENU**! Rename your first level to Main Menu, open it up, and import the sprites you created. In case if you have forgotten how to do that, click on **Images** in the **Library** and click the **+** button to import them, simple as that!

4. Arrange your actors around to create your main menu; I arranged them around to look like part of a level.

5. Create another actor and name it Text; this will be used to display text, such as the **menu title**, buttons and any copyright information you would like to include.

6. You should end up with something like the following screenshot:

7. Don't forget that when creating text actors, to set the **alpha** to 0. To do this, double-click the actor in the **Attributes**, open up the **Color** drop-down list, and change the **Alpha** value to 0. We aren't going to populate the actors with behaviors in this chapter, so let's continue.

What just happened?

In this section, we created a level that will be our main menu. You created a nice-looking background, some labels for the title and copyright info, and some buttons that we will be programming later on in this book.

Have a go hero

Create your own main menu. For this project, we are going to make a level selector, and leaderboards section for iOS; but if you're just making this game for fun, no need to do either of these. Try to make it look as snazzy as you can, this will be more appealing to people (of course).

Level selection

Go back to the project **Home** screen and create a new level, rename it to `Level Selection` or something like that. Open it up. We will now populate this level.

Create a text actor at the top of the level and change its **Display Text** behavior to **Choose your level!**. Create another text actor, double-click it and change its size to 81x81 and its **Display Text** behavior to **Level**. Click the **back** button to return to the level editor. Now, we are going to duplicate this second actor 9 times. Hold the *Option* key and click the actor to duplicate it, then align them in a grid of 5X2 for 10 levels.

 Alternatively, you can predesign everything in your favorite imaging software. Many people will do this because not only can you make everything look really nice (instead of solid colors you can do gradients), but you can also use different fonts that are not useable in GameSalad.

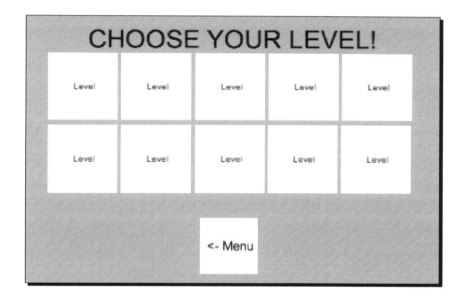

Then duplicate the actor again and drag it to the bottom middle of the level. Edit that actor and change its behavior to **<- Menu**. Don't worry that it looks bad right now, we are going to make it look much better in the next chapter by grabbing screenshots of the levels and adding the images to the buttons.

If you want, you can create a 480x320p image and draw an image for the backdrop instead of creating everything in GameSalad.

So, whatever you like to do, whatever you think looks better, go ahead.

Have a go hero

Design your own level selection screen. Create your own background if you like and make it look as cool as possible. I know you'll do an awesome job!

Creating Level 1

Let's get started in doing the most important thing, that is, creating the levels.

Time for action – creating the easy levels

Now, it's time to have some fun! We are going to start creating some levels; this first set of levels are going to be easy for the player to solve. Onward!

1. Now comes the exciting part! Go back to the project **Home** screen and create a new level, renaming it to `Level 1`. Now, double-click it and start editing this level. Do you have an idea of what you'd like to do for the level? If not, it's ok, you can do what I did.

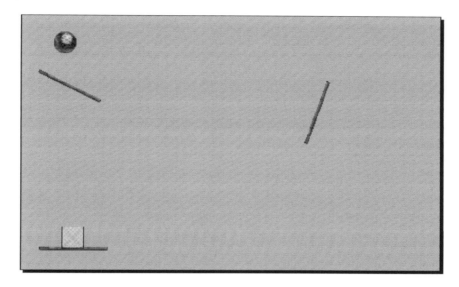

2. Drag the Ball actor into the level; place it close to the top left of the level.

3. Create a Platform actor underneath the ball and rotate it slightly, enough to bounce the ball away.

4. Create another Platform actor at the right of the level and rotate it, so it's close to a 90 degree angle but slightly off. The one in my level was set to a `71` rotation.

5. Create your last Platform actor at the bottom of the level, almost directly under the ball's original start point.

6. Create the Basket actor on the final platform.

That's it for the first level! Simple, yet requires some thinking to solve.

What the player has to do is drag the platform from the right end of the screen close to where the ball falls to make it ricochet into the basket.

What just happened?

You created your first level! Congratulations! We used the sprites we created at the beginning of this chapter and arranged them into a puzzle. This one is easy for the player to solve, but as the levels progress, it will get more difficult.

Have a go hero

Feeling creative? Try creating your own level, change the level background color or image to whatever you like, make it look pretty, and create your own awesome puzzle. Don't forget this is the first level, so it has to be creative to solve, yet simple enough for the first time players.

Creating Level 2

For this game, basically what we are going to do is make the first five levels easy, and the last five difficult. Ok, let's get to it! Go back to the project **Home** screen and create a new level, and name it Level 2, now let's double-click it to open up the scene editor.

I want this level to be in the mountains, so let's create a mountain backdrop.

Boom! There it is. Ok, now let's import that into our level.

1. Import your new image into GameSalad's image library.

2. Drag it either into the level, or into the **Inspector**; you may have to resize it to fit the level canvas.

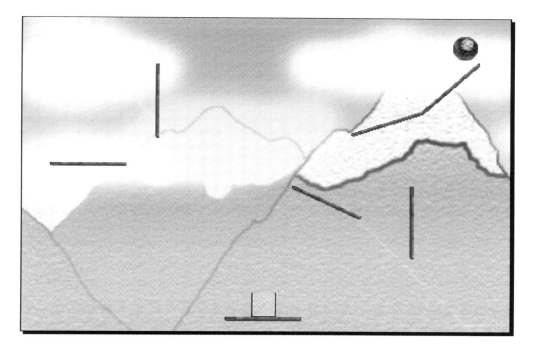

3. Drag the Ball actor to the top right of the level.

4. Create two Platform actors that will form a ramp directly underneath the ball.

5. Underneath the ramp you just created, create another ramp of one platform.

6. Create a completely vertical wall, so when the ball launches off the single ramp you just created, it will bounce off.

7. Off to the side, create a rotated platform for a wall and a straight platform. These will be the building blocks for the player to use.

To solve this puzzle, the player will have to drag the wall beside the single ramp, so the ball rolls off the big ramp, bounces off the wall, rolls down the single ramp, and hits the wall. Then the player will have to drag the regular straight platform underneath the vertical wall, so the ball will roll into the basket.

Have a go hero

Create your own version of this level; give the player two platforms to drag around to solve the puzzle. You can make it as complex as you want, just as long as it is so obvious how to solve it. On to level 3!

Creating Level 3

Now the game will start to get a little more difficult, as we are going to start creating more complex puzzles. We are going to have three platforms the player will have to move around in order to solve the puzzle.

This one is going to be on the moon!

Mmmm, it's as if you're actually there on the sea of tranquility. Let's start creating this level now. In the project **Home** screen create a new level, and name it Level 3. Double-click on it and start editing it. Import your new image into the library and drag it into the level.

1. Create the Ball actor at the top-left corner of the level.

2. Create a three platform ramp starting at a hard angle, leveling off to almost flat.

3. Leave a gap, large enough for the ball to fit through, and then continue the ramp with two or more platforms.

4. Create a flat platform underneath the gap and slightly to the left of it.

5. Create another platform, lower again, and to the far left of the level.

6. Create a flat platform that joins a ramp of one platform, below and to the right of the last platform.

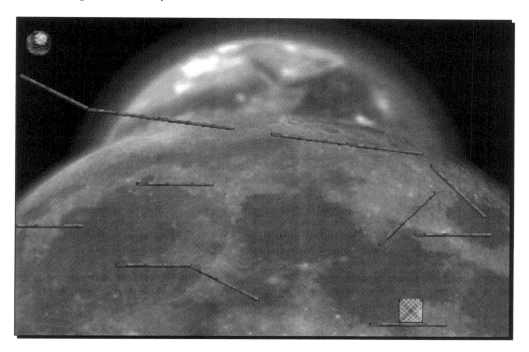

7. Then create your basket further to the right of the ramp you just created, as shown in the previous screenshot.

8. Create three platforms for the player to move around, one flat and two at opposite angles.

To solve this puzzle, the player has to stop the ball from rolling all the way down the ramp, so it falls through the gap and rolls off the platform on to the level below. The ball will have enough momentum to roll to the next platform underneath it. The player will have to drag the other angle to that platform, so the ball doesn't roll off the level and gains more momentum. The ball will then roll to the platform and ramp below, and the player will have to drag the flat platform to bridge the gap from the ramp to the basket.

Create your own version of this level, make it as cool and complex as you like; again this is your game, so make it amazing my friend!

Creating Level 4

This level is going to be near the sun!

Yep, that's a shooting cow! They're very rare, one only passes by our earth every 50,000 years. I was lucky enough to capture this image with one in it. Yeah, anyways let's create this level.

Import your new image into GameSalad's image library and drag it into your level, and resize accordingly. Then, create a new level in the project **Home** screen and name it Level 4.

This level is going to be a negative gravity level, so the ball will fall upwards instead of down, so let's build the puzzle accordingly.

1. Create the ball at the lower-left corner of the level.

2. Create an upwards ramp going to the right end of the screen of two angled platforms, and a straight platform at the end of it.

3. Where the ball would roll upwards, create an angled platform that will bounce the ball to the left; this will be just a small angle.

4. Where that platform will bounce the ball, create an opposite-angle platform sending the ball to the right, and off the screen.

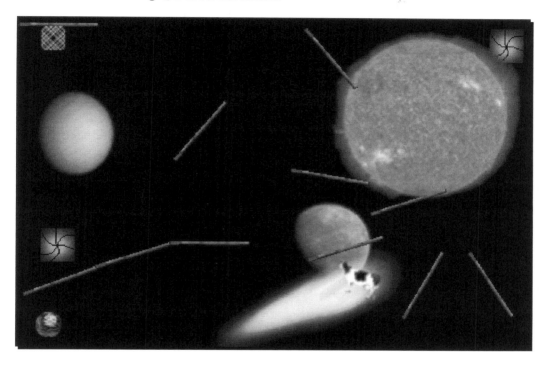

5. Create your basket directly above the ball's starting point at the top of the level.

6. Create two, 18 or 19 degree platforms for the player to use, then two extreme-angled platforms, that when put together will act as a funnel. Put these off to the side.

7. I created two vortexes or teleportation points, one at the top-right corner of the screen, and one below the basket.

To solve this puzzle, the player will have to add the two 18 degree platforms to the ramp at the bottom, then using the two extreme-angled platforms, create a funnel to the top vortex. Now, the ball will be transported to the second vortex going straight up into the basket.

Have a go hero

This is a fun level to create because of the negative gravity. You can have a lot of fun creative ways for the player to solve this one. Give it a go and see what you come up with!

Creating Level 5

This one is going to be the last of our *easier* set of levels. This level is going to incorporate **Launchers**, which are bouncy platforms that will launch the ball when they are hit. So where should this level take place? Hmm... How about in an evil genius' factory, such as the one in the following screenshot!

Menacing! Ok, let's import it into GameSalad's library and now let's create a new level in the project home screen, and rename it to Level 5.

This level is going to be complex because we are going to add some launchers, platforms that rotate when the ball hits it, launching it in the air. We will create an image for this launcher too. If you would like to create your own image, you can go ahead, or just use the one that I have included. Plus, we are going to make this a larger level, the ball will control the camera in this level. Take a look at the next screenshot; we are going to make the level look as discussed. Let's go create it, shall we?

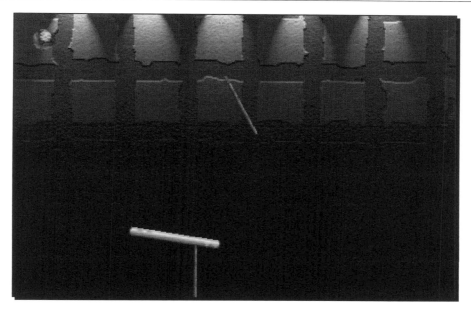

1. Create the Ball actor at the top left-hand corner of the level, as in the previous screenshot.

2. Create your Launcher actor to the right of the ball and near the bottom of the level. Also, create an angled platform for the player to use, as in the previous screenshot.

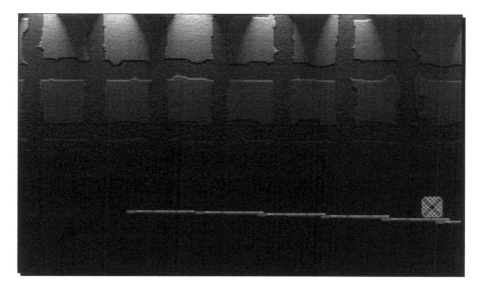

3. Scroll to the end of the level, and as in the previous screenshot, create a gradual ramp. What I did was made six flat platforms offset from each other. Then create the basket.

Solving this level is quite easy. Drag the angled platform underneath the ball so it bounces it on to the launcher. The launcher will then bounce the ball far up out of the level, and then right into the basket if done correctly.

Have a go hero

Design your own puzzle as shown previously, one that involves the use of a Launcher actor, or maybe a level that uses more than one launcher to reach the end of the level.

The past 5 levels have been fairly easy to solve, but now we are going to start some difficult levels. These ones will really make the player think long and hard about how to solve them! Let's dive right into it!

Creating Level 6

This level is going to be under water! So let's design a good underwater scene.

Bazinga! There it is. Let's create a new level in the project's home screen, and rename it to Level 6. Open it up and let's edit it.

1. Create the Ball actor at the top-left corner of the level.

2. Create a vertical tunnel using five platforms, three on the left side and two on the right.

3. Create an angled Launcher actor at the bottom of the tunnel.

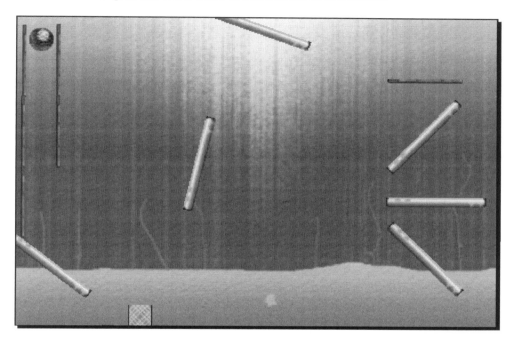

4. Create another slightly angled launcher to the right and slightly higher.

5. Create one more downward angled launcher at the top-center of the level.

6. Create a platform, and three launchers, one at a positive angle (46 degrees), a flat one, a negative angle (315 degrees), and a flat regular platform.

7. Finally, create a platform and a basket at the bottom of the level, between the first and second launchers.

To solve this, the player has to figure out the correct angle of attack, the ball will bounce differently every time. It will only take a few tries to solve this, or if the player is lucky they will get it on the first try.

Create your own version of this level; remove the chance of the same thing happening over and over by creating differently angled launchers. The ball will launch differently every time. Again, this is your game, so create your own masterpiece!

Creating Level 7, a sandbox level

What does a sandbox level mean? To solve this, the player will have to move all the platforms around to bounce the ball onto the launcher, which will bounce the flying ball to the basket. Simple enough right? It just takes some figuring out.

This level is going to be in the Sahara desert! (Get it, sandbox level, and it's in the desert.)

There it is! Filled with a sandstorm and rolling dunes.

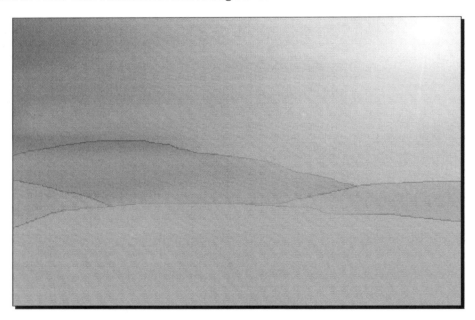

You know the drill, create a new level and rename it to Level 7. Open it up and let's edit it.

1. Create the Ball actor at the top-right corner of the level.

2. Create a Launcher actor at the bottom center of the level.

3. Now, we are going to create nine usable platforms for the user, three each of 46 degrees, 315 degrees, and 0 degrees.

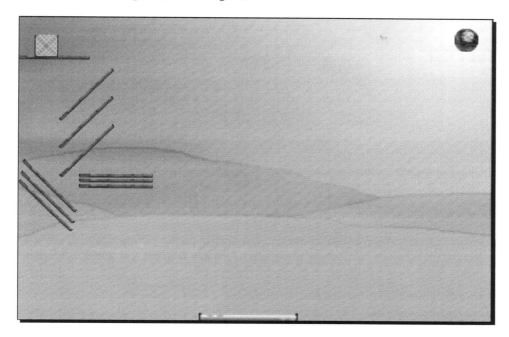

That's the level, looks filled with fun, doesn't it? In this level, we have given the player the option to create their own level, and they have the flexibility to solve it in many ways; just as long as the player can figure out how to get the ball in the basket, that's all that matters!

Have a go hero

See if you can make this more difficult; maybe add a larger level where you have to bounce the ball on to numerous launchers to reach the basket.

Creating Level 8

This level is going to be in a volcano!

Ok, there we are, a nice hot volcano with some glowing embers flying away.

[In the next chapter, we will make some actual particle embers fly around.]

Let's create this level!

1. Create a new level in the project **Home** screen, and rename it Level 8. Open it up, so we can edit it.

2. Add your new image background to the **Library** and create a new actor with the image. You may need to resize it accordingly because we selected **resolution independence**.

3. Create a Ball actor at the upper-left corner.

4. Under the Ball actor, create an angled platform (to get a perfect angle every time, when rotating press and hold the *shift* button) and a flat platform at the bottom of the angled platform.

5.   Underneath the platform you just created, create another flat platform and a vertical platform to the right.

6.   Create another angled platform and flat platform under and to the left, almost at the bottom of the level. Make sure you leave a gap for the ball to fall between the flat platform and the vertical platform created earlier.

7.   Create an angled launcher (315 degrees) directly below the gap.

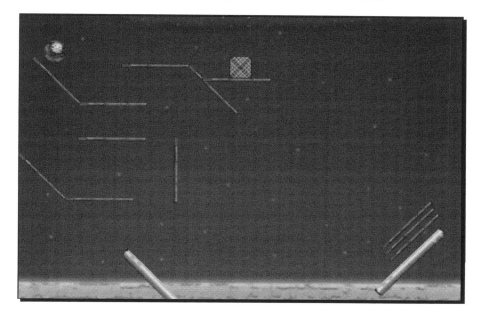

8.   Create a 45 degree launcher and three platforms at the same angle, and put them off to the side for the player to use.

9.   At the top of the level, to the right of the ball's starting point, create a flat platform with the finishing basket on it.

To solve this puzzle, the player has to divert the ball, so it doesn't fall into the lava pit at the very beginning. When it leaves the ramp, the player must put the angled platform at the end of the flat platform, so that the ball falls to the platform below. The ball will continue and fall on the ramp below. Then, it will fall into the gap and land on the launcher. The player must move the launcher to bounce the ball up to the basket, and use the remaining platforms to get the ball in the basket.

See what you can do with this level, create a difficult puzzle for the player to solve.

Onto level 9! We are on the final stretch!

Creating a very tough level, Level 9

This level is going to be on Mars! Let's start editing this level. We are on the second last level, so let's make it a difficult one.

I had to put the rover in there, and yes, he looks like a famous movie character. So let's import this image into GameSalad and create a new level and name it Level 9.

1. Create the Ball actor at the top center of the level.
2. Create two vertical platforms, forming a tunnel.
3. Then, create two more below that tunnel but leave a gap large enough for the ball to fit through.

4. Create a launcher at the bottom of the tunnels.

5. Create a box at the top-left corner of the level; at the bottom of the box leave a gap large enough for the ball to fit through.

6. Put the basket in the box, and above the gap. Create an angled platform, so when the ball hits it, it will bounce right off the screen and miss the basket. Take a look at the next screenshot to see what I mean. See the basket in the upper-left corner?

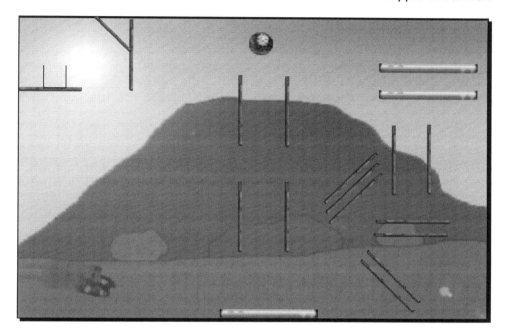

7. Now, create a bunch of usable platforms for the player to use. Two or three of different angles each, and two launchers.

The player will have to move around all the platforms to reach the basket, then when they do reach the end, they will have to block the ball from flying off the screen.

See if you can make this level a little more difficult, maybe requiring full use of platforms or having no platforms in the level make it as difficult as you can, but save your creativity for the last level because you're going to need it.

Onto level 10!

Creating Level 10

This is going to be your level to design; I'm not going to design this one. Let your creative juices flow, make it as difficult and creative as possible. The only thing I will do for you is give you a backdrop to use. This one is going to be at a concert!

The stage is set my friend, wow the crowd, you can do it! This is the last level, make it memorable, and make it rewarding, so that the player wants to play the game again just for that final satisfying end.

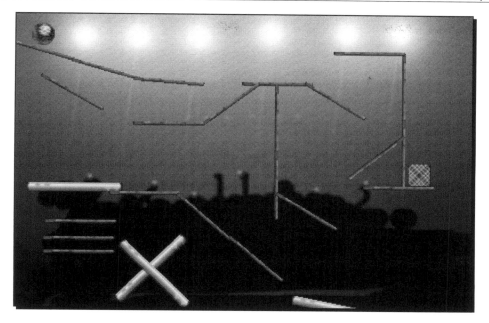

The previous screenshot is of the level I created, and now that we have finished all the levels, we have to do a final 'you won' screen, along with a screen that will show us **Game Center Leaderboards**.

The finishing touches

We are going to create the final **You Won** screen. In it, we are going to congratulate the player, show their final score, and maybe even put in some credits because after all, you want people to know who made this masterpiece.

Create a new level in the project's **Home** screen, and name it `You Win` or something similar. Design your background image as shown:

Let's add it into our library and then into our level. Once this is done, create a text actor in the area under **Final Score**. This will be our text actor that will display the score, but for now, we don't have an attribute set up yet so we will leave it blank. Add another text actor; this will be our button that will take us back to the main menu. Change the **Display text** behavior to **<- Main Menu**, or you can create an image for the button.

Have a go hero

Create your own **Congratulations** level; make it look snazzy and attractive to the eyes.

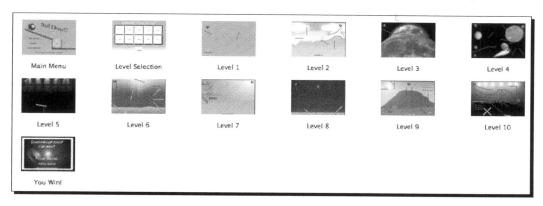

By now, how can you not love GameSalad? We are starting to learn more and more about designing games, and by the end of the next chapter, you are going to have a fully-fledged game that is ready for deployment on iOS devices, or Android! It's so exciting, isn't it? But for now, I suggest you take a break, have a nice coffee, or a nap. We have a lot more work to do, and we are just getting started.

Summary

In this chapter, we got a good feel for the GameSalad UI, including the moving, rotating, and scaling (or resizing) of actors within GameSalad. We now have all levels designed; in the next chapter, we are going to finish the game by adding behaviors, sound effects, gravity, and physics to the levels. Then to finish it all off, we are going to add touch controls (that's right, touch, not mouse controls); so if you want, you can test it on your iPhone, iPod Touch, iPad, or certain Android devices!

5
Starting Simple: Ball Drop Part 2

In the previous chapter, when we put together our Ball Drop game, we designed all the levels and images. In this chapter, we are going to finish the game by adding all the behaviors, sound effects, and more. This is where the game comes together and we add the breath of life to our work.

Ok, enough with the chit chat! What we are going to do in this chapter:

◆ Create 10 playable levels, and a menu system

◆ Add touch controls

◆ Add gravity, physics, and collisions

◆ Add behaviors to our images

◆ Add scoring and leaderboards

By the end of this chapter, you are going to have your very own work of art, everything in the game will be in working order, and it will be ready for distribution.

Let's get to it!

Creating our menu, by adding behaviors to images!

When was the last time you turned on a game and was immediately thrown into the first level, not knowing what to do? I can't think of any that I have played. Menus are very important for the player because in the menu, you as the developer can tell the player how to play, and give them a wide array of options; in iOS, for example, touch or tilt controls and in-game music or iPod music. The menu acts as a lobby for the player; when they aren't playing, they go to the menu, to take a break from playing and check out their achievements and how they stacked up on the Leaderboards. So, let's program the menu for our game.

Time for action – programming our menu

In this section, we are going to create our menu system, which involves simply adding behaviors to images. Let's dive into it...

1. Open up the **Main Menu** scene and start editing it. Double-click the actor with the text label **Play Game**, then click the button **Create Rule**.

2. Change the rule to **Actor receives event | touch | is | pressed**.

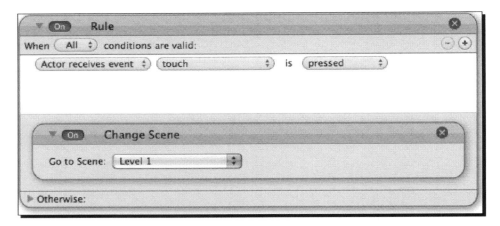

3. Add a **Change Scene** behavior into the rule, and change it to Level 1; we do this because if it were set to **Next Scene**, it would go to the **Level Selection** screen! We don't want that, not yet anyways.

4. Go back to the scene editor and double-click the actor with the label **Levels** and let's add the same rule and behavior from the previous label.

5. Change the rule to **Actor receives events | touch | is | pressed** then add in a **Change Scene** behavior, and change it to **Next Scene**.

6. Finally, we are going to set up our Leaderboards.

 Leaderboards are only available to those who have a paid, professional membership with GameSalad.

7. Double-click the **Leaderboards** button, add a **Game Center – Login** behavior, and add a new rule. Change it again to **Actor receives event | touch | is | pressed** and add a **Game Center – Show Leaderboard**. Change the **Leaderboard ID** to the ID you set up in iTunes Connect. Refer to the next screenshot to see what I mean. If you don't know how to do this, refer to the Appendix.

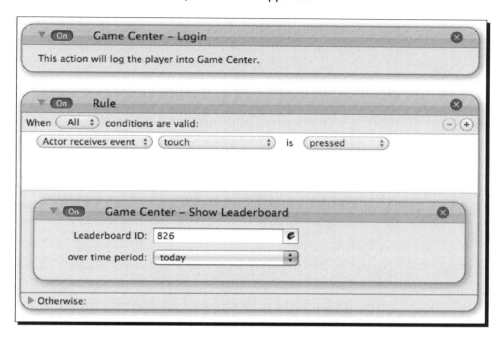

Wasn't it easy to create our menu? We added some touch controls to the button, and behaviors to follow the touch.

Time for action – creating our level selection menu

Our level selection scene is looking pretty bland right now, isn't it? We should add some images to these buttons, and what would look better than the actual screenshots of the levels? That's what we are going to do next!

1. Open up your first level, click the **Preview** button, and then click on the button with the camera icon in the upper-right toolbar to take a screenshot.

2. Click the **Save...** button to save the current shot as a file. Repeat this step for all the levels, I know it's not fun but hey, it looks great.

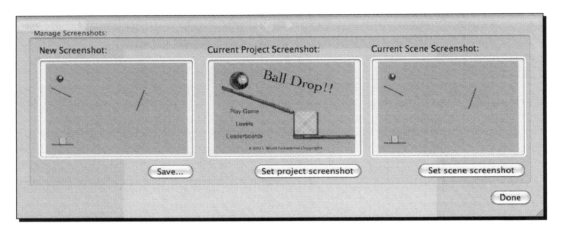

3. Then import the images to the **Library** and drag them on to the appropriate button. They may not fit properly within the frame we made, so just resize them accordingly.

4. Now, we have to add behaviors to the buttons. Simply click the button you want, click **Create Rule**, change the middle property from **Actor receives event | mouse button | is | down** to **Actor receives event | touch | is | pressed**. Then drag a **Change Scene** behavior into the rule and change **Go to scene:** to the level you want. Repeat for all the other buttons.

You can click **Rule** and press *command + C* to copy the whole rule, then press *command + V* to paste it into the other buttons, saving a lot of time, or you can click *Option* and select **Behaviors** for an even faster method!)

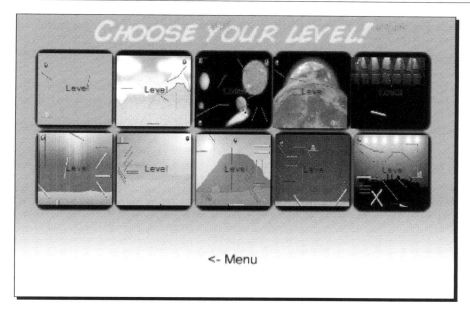

5. Test to see if you did them right; click **Preview** and make sure the button sends the player to the right level, small mistakes like this can ruin your app. It's a good thing that I double-checked them because I put the wrong images for four of the buttons!

6. Finally, program the **Menu** button. Double-click it and repeat what you did with the rest of the buttons, but change **Go to scene:** to the **Menu** scene.

That's it for this level!

What just happened?

In this section, we learned how to create screenshots for each level and create some buttons with images on them. Creating these screenshots is very helpful for submitting your game to iTunes or even posting some images on your website or on Facebook.

Programming the first five levels

We are going to start with programming the first five levels; we are going to do touch controls, physics, and collisions, so let's get to it.

Creating Level 1

This is the first level, so we are going to make it easy but still interesting.

1. Double-click your player actor in the **Inspector** (to edit the main prototype or the original actor). Under the **Physics** roll-out, change the **Restitution** to 0.5, then drag in two **Collide** behaviors. Change the actors to Platform and Flinger.

> **Restitution**: The return to an original physical condition, especially after elastic deformation. In other words, bounciness.

2. Next add a rule, change it to **Actor receives event | overlaps or collides | with actor of type | Basket**, add a **Change Scene** behavior, and set it to **Next Scene**. We will add more behaviors as we go on, but for now that's all we need.

Time for action – adding gravity, touch controls, and physics

Let's start with the gravity. Go back to **Level 1**.

1. Add the **Gravity** to the scene in the **Inspector**, then click the **Scene** button and expand the **Gravity** roll-out and change **Y** to 300.

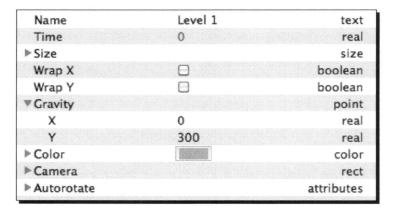

Name	Level 1	text
Time	0	real
▶ Size		size
Wrap X	☐	boolean
Wrap Y	☐	boolean
▼ Gravity		point
X	0	real
Y	300	real
▶ Color		color
▶ Camera		rect
▶ Autorotate		attributes

2. Next, we are going to start programming the **Useable Platforms,** the ones that the player will be using to move around to solve the puzzles. To do this, we are going to create some touch controls and physics.

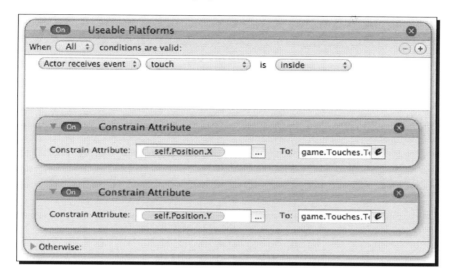

3. Double-click the platform which the player will move around. Now you'll see a big lock where you put the behaviors; click that because we only want to edit this specific platform, not all of them.

4. Under the **Physics** roll-out, change the **Restitution** to 0.5. Create a rule and name it Useable Platforms, then change the attributes to **Actor receives event | touch | is | inside**. Then, as shown in the previous screenshot, drag in two **Constrain Attribute** behaviors. For the first one, we are going to do **Constrain Attribute: | self.Position.X | To: | game.Touches.Touch 1.X**. The second will be the same, but instead of **X** we are going to use **Y**.

We use **touch inside** because it detects the touch within the actor only when the player is touching that specific actor.

5. You may need to resize the actor to make it easier for the player. If this is the case, double-click the actor, then click the **Graphics** roll-out and change **Horizontal/Vertical Wrap** to **Fixed**. This allows you to stretch the size of the actor without stretching the image itself. Also, don't forget to uncheck the **Moveable** option in the **Physics Attributes**; if we don't, all the platforms will fall! Now, to save ourselves a lot of time, click the **Custom** button in the **Library**, and drag the whole rule into the **Custom** behaviors.

Test the level to see if everything works, if so, wonderful! Now, you should start making it a habit to save every time you incorporate some new changes. This is a good practice because sometimes (not always) you can experience a crash in GameSalad and you will lose a lot of important work.

What just happened?

In this section, we looked at how to add gravity to the level; the value can be any amount that you want. If you want, you can even use a negative number for negative gravity such as in space. Then we saw how to create touch controls for our useable platforms. The moment a player touches them, they will follow their touch.

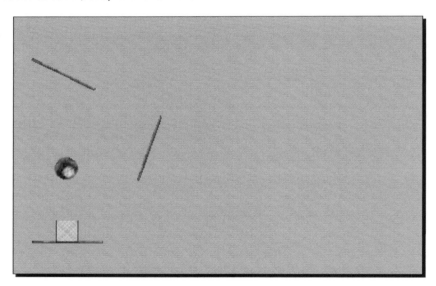

Creating Level 2

Time to finish creating this level. We have the canvas all drawn up now, we have to "color it in", and by that I mean adding the behaviors to our actors.

1. Open up the second level and change **Gravity** to 300.

2. Double-click the two platforms that are going to be useable. Go to your **Custom** behaviors, and drag **Useable Platforms** into the behaviors of the actor.

3. Test it to make sure everything works well.

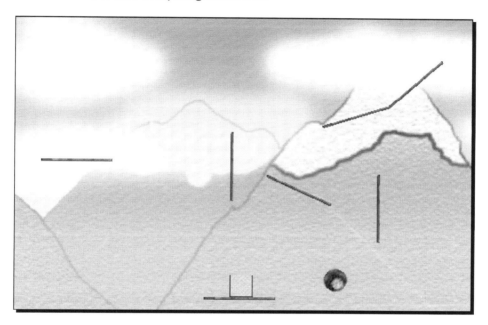

Oops, I didn't do it right! As you can see from the previous screenshot, I was unable to pass the level.

Creating Level 3

This level takes place on the moon, so we are going to have less gravity. Let's get to it.

1. Open up the third level. Don't forget this is our moon level, so we are going to do less gravity; let's change **Y** to 100.

2. Now add the **Useable Platform** behavior to the three platforms that the player is going to use.

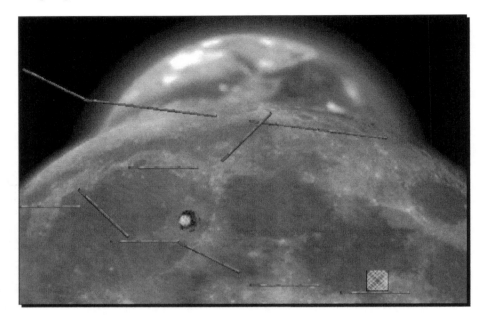

Creating Level 4

This is going to be a fun level to create because we are going to have negative gravity (in other words, you will go up instead of down), and there will also be some teleporters!

Time for action – programming teleporters

Now, we are going to make the teleporters. Don't worry, they are easy to make!

1. This level is a negative gravity level, so let's change **Y** to -100 and add the behaviors to the four platforms that the player will use.

2. Double-click the ball actor in the current scene and add a new rule.

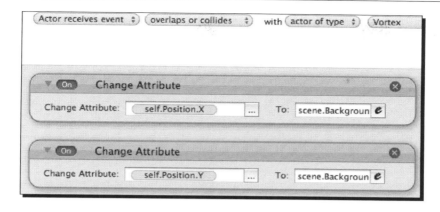

3. Change the attribute to **Actor receives events | overlaps or collides | with actor of type Vortex** and add two **Change Attribute** behaviors, one for **X** and other for **Y**. Change the first one to **self.Position.X | to: | scene.Background.Vortex.Position.X** and repeat for **Y**, but use the Y position instead.

4. Test to make sure you chose the right vortex, if not, go back to the behavior and select the right vortex in the scene.

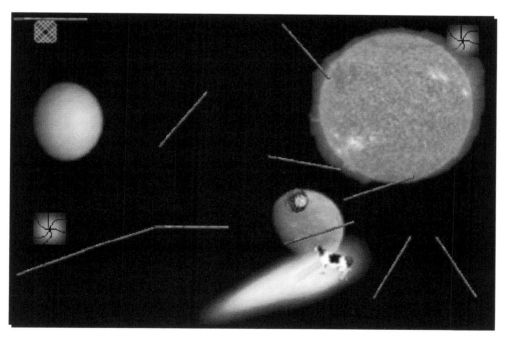

What just happened?

Using GameSalad's powerful attributes, we were able to easily create two vortex/worm holes that teleport the ball from one part of the level to the other. This technique can be used in any type of game, and it can also be used to create a teleporting boss that appears at random areas! Ooh scary! Let's keep going!

Creating Level 5

This is the level where we use bouncy platforms! Also, this is going to be a long level, so we are going to incorporate scrolling with the camera!

Time for action – side scrolling

Side scrolling games are some of the most enjoyable games out there (in my opinion anyways), how do they do it? Well, programming it is a huge task, but with GameSalad it's so easy! It's just a matter of creating a large level (anything more than the viewable screen size; the iPhone's screen for example is 320x480) and then drag the Player actor. The following steps show how it is done:

1. Bouncy time! Ok, let's get to it! Double-click the ball actor in the scene, add a **Control Camera** behavior, go back to the scene editor, click the **Camera Mode** button, as shown in the following screenhsot:

2. Now, move the bounds of the camera so that they are in the center, as shown in the following screenshot:

3. Now, as in the rest of the levels, you have to add the **Useable Platforms** behavior to the platform the player will be using, and also change the **Gravity** to 300.

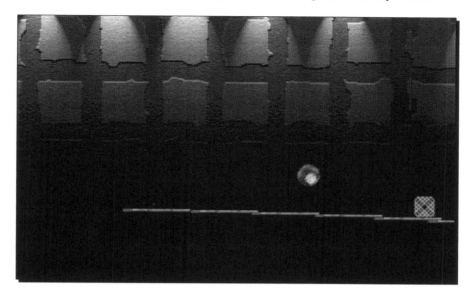

Everything works and looks great! Do you want to take a break?

What just happened?

In these first five levels, we were able to take a look at some different, more complex behaviors, such as constraining attributes (like the platforms' X and Y value to a touch), removing the bounciness of an object by lowering its **Restitution**, switching levels via collisions, teleporting, and changing the position of an object when it collides with another. We also looked at how to make an object control the camera with a simple behavior! It's so easy, isn't it?

Go ahead, take a breather, go get a coffee, and a doughnut. Mmmmm honey cruller, no Boston cream! Ugh! I'll just get a dozen assorted. We can pick this up when you get back.

Creating the last five levels

How was your break? Mine was great, but I had to change because I dropped a jelly doughnut on my white shirt. Now we are going to start programming our more complex levels. Don't worry, they are going to be hard to solve, but not hard to program! Let's get into it!

Creating Level 6

This is the underwater level so we are going to have more gravity.

1. Open up the sixth level and change the **Gravity** to 400.

2. Add our **Useable Platforms** behaviors to the first platform and three launchers, which the player will be able to use. I forgot to mention one thing, change the **Restitution** of the launchers to 1.5, to make them slightly more bouncy.

3. Test the level to make sure everything works well and you're comfortable with the restitution of the launchers, and save your work.

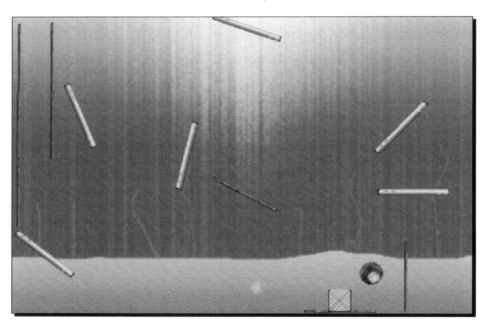

Everything was good for me, but I did have to rotate some of the launchers around, and I had to add a wall beside the basket to prevent the ball from flying off the screen, but in the end, I was able to solve the puzzle. Just to make this level look a little better, why not add an actor over the top of the level, blue and slightly transparent, that emits particles for bubbles.

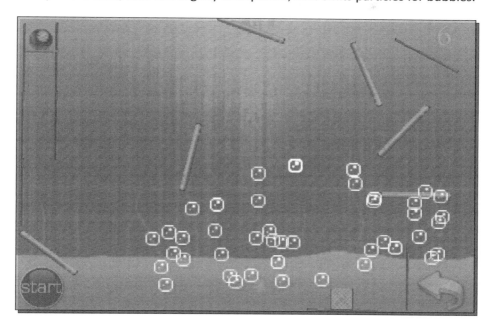

Creating Level 7

This level is going to be a blank canvas, in other words, we aren't going to create a puzzle for the players to solve, they will create their own. We are going to give the player a blank level and all the pieces to solve it.

1. All you have to do for this level is add the **Useable Platforms** behavior to the nine platforms that are set up for the user. Double-click the nine platforms created in the previous chapter and drag in our custom **Useable Platforms** behavior.

2. Add a **Gravity** of 300 to the scene, as with the rest of the levels. Then once you have done that don't forget to test your level to make sure it's solvable.

3. What we originally designed can differ slightly as compared to the finished product. When we were designing it, we couldn't test it, so we didn't know if it would work 100 percent, but as you can see in the next screenshot, everything worked perfectly. On to level 8!

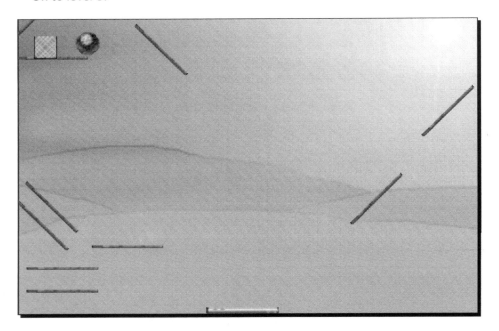

Creating Level 8

This is going to be a very cool-looking level, we are going to create some cool-looking particle effects, and some platforms that will kill our ball and reset the level. Change the **Gravity** of the level to 200, there will be less gravity in this level because of the intense heat of the volcano. Create an actor and name it Particles, resize the actor to the width of the level, or more if you want, and move it to the bottom of the scene.

Time for action – adding particles and kill zones

As mentioned, we are going to create some particle effects and "kill zones" (platforms that will kill you when you land on them). Plus, they are going to be on fire! Cool! So what you need to do is:

1. Double-click the **Particle** actor, and add **Particles** behavior. Let's change the settings to the following:

    - **Number of Particles:** 100
    - **Particle Startup Time:** 2
    - **Particle Lifetime:** 20
    - **Emitter Offset:** random(-300, 480)
    - **Direction:** 90
    - **Speed:** 20
    - **Size:** 2
    - **Color:** Orange
    - **Blending:** Additive
    - **Angular Velocity:** 10

2. Now, you have to add the **Useable Platforms** behavior to the three platforms and one launcher that the user will be moving around. Select a couple of the immobile platforms and copy the same particle effect into the behaviors.

    - **Number of Particles:** 100
    - **Particle Startup Time:** 2
    - **Particle Lifetime:** 1.5
    - **Emitter Offset:** random(-30, 30)
    - **Direction:** 90
    - **Speed:** 20
    - **Size:** 2
    - **Color:** Orange
    - **Blending:** Additive
    - **Angular Velocity:** 10

3. Then add another rule, and change the rule to **Actor receives event | overlaps or collides | with actor of type | Ball** and add a **Reset Scene** behavior into the rule. Copy that rule into the **Particle** actor, so when the ball flies off into the lava the scene will reset.

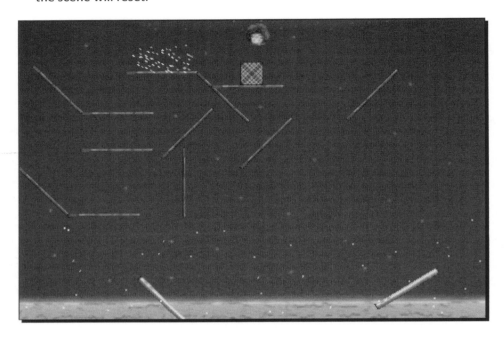

As you can see, it works! And the level looks good with those particles flying around.

What just happened?

We discussed how to create particle effects, like the ones in the previous screenshot. These are just embers and flames, but GameSalad's particle system is so powerful that you can do anything from rain, to fire, to shrapnel, you can even do things like magic effects and waterfalls. We also looked at how we can kill a player when they land on certain platforms; of course these can be used to destroy our character when they get outside of the level bounds, or when they land on spikes, or in lava!

Creating Level 9

Let's add all the behaviors to the platforms the player is going to use—nine regular wooden platforms and two launcher platforms. Look at the following screenshot to see how I arranged them. This level was kind of tricky to test, it took me a few times to get it right but it works just fine, once you have all the pieces properly put together. The **Gravity**, as in most of the other levels is going to be 300.

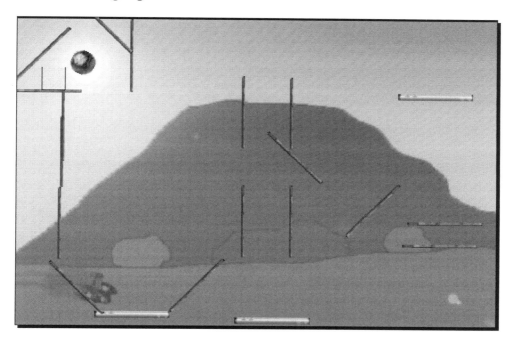

Creating Level 10

This level is going to be designed by you. Don't follow my design; try making your own puzzle. For now, the following screenshot is what I created and we will use it as a guide.

1. This is it! The final level! But we're not done quite yet, we need to put the behaviors into the three platforms and two launchers for the player to use.

2. Now, as with all levels, you have to test to see if any adjustments are needed. As you can see in the next screenshot, I needed to do a few. In the long run, it did end up working but it took me a few tries to get it right.

Now we have to add the scoring and HUD's.

Creating the finishing touches

Our game is looking great, isn't it? We are going to spice it up even more though, by creating some scoring (so that we can later upload to Game Center Leaderboards) and a HUD, which will be two buttons that allow the player to start the level, and reset it. Let's dive in!

Time for action – scoring, HUD, and more!

Now, we are going to add some important information, such as the score—which will be a timer—and the name of the person who beat the game in the least amount of time, which will be uploaded to the Game Center Leaderboards.

1. Open the first level, and in the **Inspector** with the **Game** button selected, click the **Attributes** tab. Click the **+** button and when the **Pick an Attribute Type:** dialog pops up, select **Integer**. You will see a **New Attribute** in the **Inspector**. Rename it to Time.

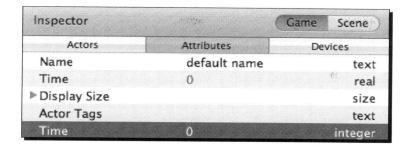

2. Click the **Actors** tab again and create a new actor and name it **Time**. Now, we are going to edit this actor, so double-click it and let's get to it.

3. Add a **Display Text** behavior, and click the little **e** beside the text field, then add **Game | Time**, change the alignment to the last one, which is to the right of the actor. Now, change the size to something decent, I used **Georgia** with a **Size** 20.

4. Don't forget to change the **Alpha** to 0, and the **Moveable** option to off because we don't want this to fall off the screen.

 In case you've forgotten with all our platform objects we want to uncheck the **Moveable** option, otherwise they will fall right off the screen due to the gravity!

5. Now, we are going to add a timer behavior, change it to **Every** 1 **Seconds**, and add a **Change Attribute** behavior. Change the first setting to **game.Time | To: | game. Time + 1**, and this will increase the time by one every second.

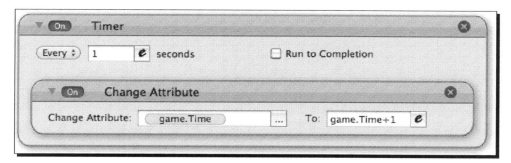

Now, in every level, add this actor to the upper-right corner of the level.

Alternatively, you can add a **Spawn Actor** behavior within the **Ball** actor and have it placed at the top of the screen. This will save a lot of time because you won't have to go into each level to create and position this actor by hand.

Now, we have to add a few more things. We need to add a gate that will stop the ball from falling, then we need to make a button such that once the player has arranged all their useable platforms, they can then press it to start the ball rolling.

What just happened?

In this section, we set up a level timer, which we will use to calculate the scores and we also added some additional HUD actors.

Allowing the player time to think

It wouldn't be fair for the player, if the moment they open the level, the ball starts falling right away. So in this section, we are going to fix that by creating a gate that will stop the ball from falling. When the player is ready, they can tap a button that will destroy the gate, allowing the ball to fall.

Time for action – starting and restarting the level with buttons

With this section, we are going to create a way for the player to take time to look at the level, moving all the pieces around to solve it. As mentioned previously, we are going to create a gate that will stop the ball from falling, then a button that when tapped, will destroy the ball. Made a mistake? That's ok! We are going to create another button that will restart the level. Let's go!

1. Go to the first level and in the **Inspector**, create a new actor and name it Gate or something along those lines. Use whatever image you want for it, I am going to use the launcher image but I am going to change its color. Then, change its **Restitution** to 0, and the **Friction** to 20, as you don't want the ball to bounce and roll off.

2. Then double-click the **Ball** actor and add a **Collide** behavior and change it to **Gate**. So let's go ahead and add this actor underneath the ball in each level.

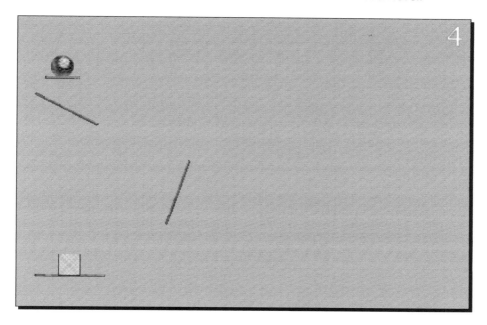

3. Now, we have to add a button that will destroy that gate. Go back to **level 1** and in the **Inspector**, create a new actor and name it Start Button. In the **Attributes**, click the **+** button and when the dialogue appears select **Boolean** (a Boolean is a simple true or false statement) and name the Boolean Start.

4. Now, double-click the new actor to edit it. Change its size by setting **Width** to 50 and **Height** to 50. Download or create an image for that button, preferably something big and shiny that says 'start' on it.

5. Now, create a rule in the **Start Button** actor and change the rule to **Actor receives event | touch | is | pressed**. Drag a **Change Attribute** behavior into the rule, change it to **Change Attribute: | game.Start | To: | true**, then expand the **Otherwise** roll-out and copy the **Change Attribute** behavior into the **Otherwise** section. Change this attribute to **false** instead of **true**. Basically, what this does is that when the button is clicked, that Boolean will be true but as soon as the player releases it, it will change back to false.

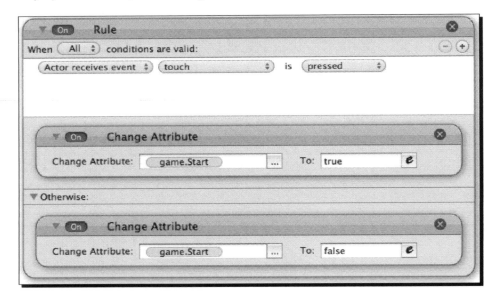

6. Now let's go back to the scene editor. We need to edit the **Gate** actor, so double-click it. Add a new rule to it and change it to **Attribute | game.Start | is | true**, then we need to add in a **Destroy Actor** behavior. Now just drag in your button into the level and test it out!

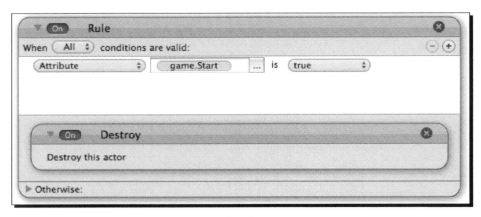

7. If it works, don't forget to save your project!

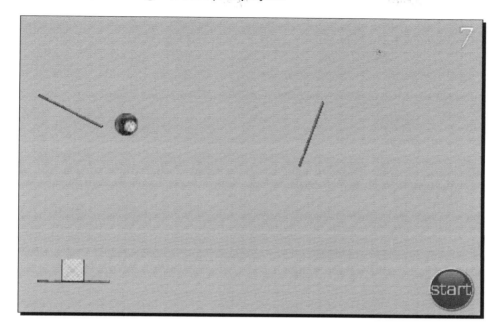

8. Seems like it does! If it did work, just drag in the button actor into every level. But wait a minute, when the ball falls off the screen, nothing happens! Okay, we are going to add another button that will restart the level.

9. Let's go back to the scene editor, so we can make a new actor, name this one `Reset` and double-click it to edit it.

10. Change the size by setting **Height** to `50` and **Width** to `50` and again grab or create an image for it. Now, create a new rule for the reset button, and change it to **Actor receives event | touch | is | pressed** then drag in a **Reset Level** behavior.

That's it! Test the game to make sure everything is working properly. If not, take your time and go back to make sure you did everything correctly. Now, we just have to finish one last thing: the final score, and uploading it to Game Center.

What just happened?

In this section, we created a system to allow the player to think. Instead of the ball falling as soon as you start the level, we created a gate to stop the ball from falling to give them time to look around the level. We created a button to destroy that gate and another to restart the level in case the player makes a mistake.

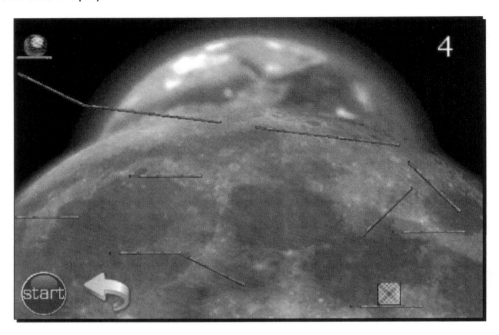

Top Score and Game Center

1. Go to our final level, not the playable one but the You Win screen. Find the one **text** actor that currently shows **Hello World** and double-click it to edit it. In the **Display Text** behavior, click the **e** beside the text field and select **Game | Time**. Now this will show the score!

2. Now, we want to upload it. Again, this is only for Pro members. If you are not one, you can skip this, but I would suggest upgrading because it is a fantastic package.

3. Drag in a Game Center's **Post Score** behavior. Where it says **Post Attribute** select **game.Time** and in the **Leaderboard ID** type in your Leaderboard ID that you chose when setting up your Leaderboard within iTunes Connect, as shown in the next screenshot. (Refer to the Appendix for more information).

At the time of editing this book, version 0.9.91 of GameSalad was released, and it included new features for Pro members only, such as Tables, IAPs or in-app purchases, monetization from Kiip and PlayHaven. They always make it worth your while to upgrade to Pro if you are able to afford it.

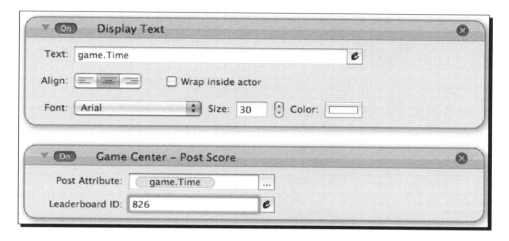

If you did everything right, you should see the following screenshot when you get to this level:

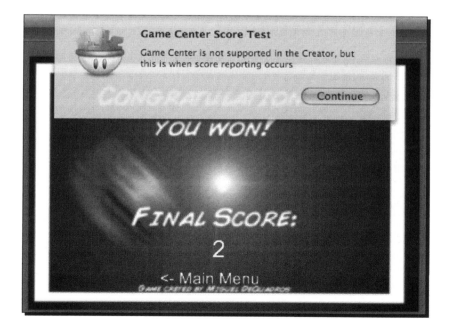

Don't forget to add a rule to the **Main Menu** button on that screen, and have it go to the main menu level.

And that's it my friends! That's how easy it is to make a simple and fun game. Yes it took a while to create it but the creation is half the fun! The other half of the fun is seeing your friends' faces as they see your very own game on the App Store! Are you ready to test it on your device or send it to Apple for review? On your project's home screen, click the **Publish** button.

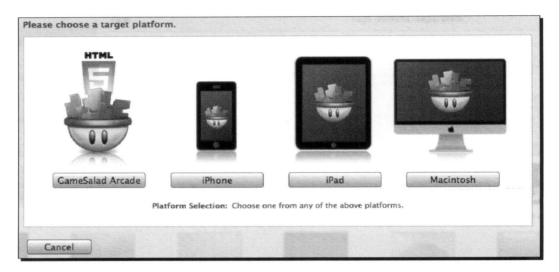

Choose your platform, which in this case would be iPhone, then follow the on screen prompts and voila! Your game is ready to go! From here, you can drag it into iTunes or Xcode, install the app on your device, or log in to www.itunesconnect.apple.com to upload it to Apple for reviews to upload into the App Store!

Congratulations! You just made an awesome game! You learned how to add various behaviors for added functionality, you added buttons that do a wide array of things, you added a few obstacles to kill the player, but you can add more! You can make this game truly your game!

 For levels that are large and require scrolling, there is a neat feature called Layers in GameSalad. In the **Inspector**, click the **Scene** button, and the **Layers** tab, and from here you can add as many layers as you want, and also choose if you want them to scroll with the rest of the level. If you uncheck **scrollable**, it will follow the screen, which is great for buttons, score labels, and anything else.

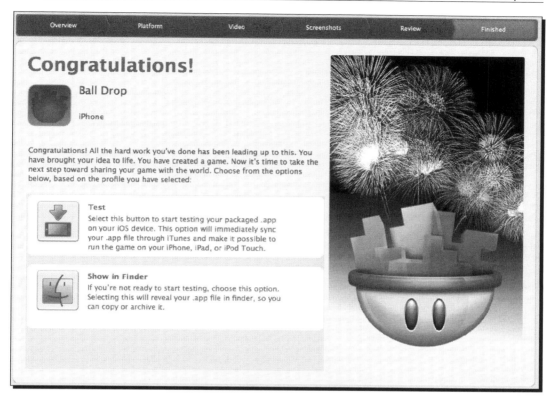

Pop quiz

1. How do you take a screenshot of your level?

   a. Press **Print Screen**

   b. *Command + Shift + 3*

   c. When testing click the **Camera** button

   d. When testing hold *Shift + S* key

2. How do you constrain an actor to a touch?

   a. Add a **Collide with Touch** behavior

   b. Add a **Touch Movement** behavior

   c. Create a rule that detects the players touch and constrain X,Y to touch

   d. None of the above

3. How do you show Leaderboards?

   a. Add a **Show Leaderboard** Behavior to a button

   b. Get a Pro membership

   c. Both of the above

   d. Neither of the above

Summary

Congratulations! You've created another game! Except that this one was more complex in its programming, we created touch controls, collisions, and physics. We also looked at a timer, which we used for our score; the less time it takes, the higher in the Game Center Leaderboards you will be. Are you having fun yet? Well, in the next chapter, we are going to have even more fun; we are going to create a game called **Space Defender**, which is an Asteroids clone, with multiple enemies, touch controls, and we will even deploy our game to our devices to test it. We will create spaceship movement, better looking sprites, and more!

Are you as excited as I am? Well, let's get into it, shall we?

6
Space Defender Part 1

How was your break? I hope it was good! Anyways, remember back in 1979 when times were easier? When the best game on the market was a simple 2D single-colored set of pixels flying around a CRT screen? Yes in 1979, Atari released arguably the most influential game in history, Asteroids. I never saw the '70s or most of the '80s but I played Asteroids, as has the majority of the world and it is quite an addictive game. It's one of those great games where you and a group of friends would play for hours to see who could get the high score. What does that have to do with this chapter? We are going to make an Asteroids clone, but we are going to have some better-looking effects. After all, our game is going to be on the iPhone!

This game is going to be a little more complex than our last one. We are going to incorporate some more touch controls via buttons to control the ship, include various enemies, and at the end of this chapter we are going to deploy our game to the iPhone for testing purposes, which will help immensely when getting your game ready to deploy to the App Store. You will get to see how it performs and controls on the device. Nothing would be worse than releasing a game that doesn't work! Let's see what we are going to cover in this chapter:

◆ Creating a good user interface and sprites

◆ Numerous AI (enemies)

◆ Sound effects

◆ Spaceship movement

Things are going to get juicy in this chapter, and by the end, you are going to have a great idea of how to effectively use GameSalad's more complex procedures. As with the last game, this is going to be divided into two chapters because there is a lot to cover and you need to breathe in between. Let's go!

Creating UI and sprites

I think, for this chapter, I am going to use Photoshop to design all the sprites. Let's start with the **Logo Screen**; this is simply going to be a screen that shows your company logo or a logo to represent yourself. I have a company, so following is the logo that I'm going to use for this game.

 If the images imported into Game Salad are smaller than your actual image (for example, you import an image at 960x640 and it imports at 240x160) then, while saving your image, make sure your resolution is 72DPI that is, 72 dots per inch. Then, import it into GameSalad and you will have the correct resolution.

Ooh... pretty! This is exactly what the player wants to see! The previous screenshot is a flashy, cool-looking graphic, but don't forget that it has to match your gameplay. Ok, so let's import that into GameSalad, create a new project, and fill in all the details on the main screen.

1. Now, open up your **Initial Scene** and start editing it.

2. Import your image into the **Library** and drag it into your scene. All we are going to do with this actor is add a **Timer** behavior, so double-click it (the actor), drag in a **Timer** behavior and change its attribute to **Every** 4 **seconds**, and drag in a **Change Scene** behavior and set it to **Next Scene**.

3. If you want to have more than one of these splash screens, then by all means do it; I did it too.

4. Just copy the first level, change the image, and keep the timer the same. Now, let's move on to our **Main Menu**; create a super flashy looking background for this one. As for me, I am going to imitate the original Asteroids box art.

It's pretty easy to create splash screens, isn't it?

Creating the menu and more sprites

Now that we are done with our company logos, we are going to create the menu.

1. Add a new actor, and name it Text Button or something similar. Drag it into the middle of the level and double-click to edit it.

2. Add a new rule to the actor, change it to **Actor receives event | touch | is | pressed;**; then add a **Change Scene** behavior to the rule and change its setting to **Next Scene**.

3. Then add a **Display Text** behavior, and change the text to Tap to Play. For now, this is going to be the only button we add; but in the next chapter, we will add some more.

4. Create a new level and name it Level, this is going to be our playground for our spaceship to save the world. Next, we have to design the sprites:

Our background: Following is a cool background screenshot for our level, lots of stars, and some space dust floating around.

The asteroid: Following is a screenshot for the asteroid, nothing too fancy but it still looks like an asteroid.

Player spaceship: Following is a screenshot for your spaceship, it looks pretty cool, doesn't it? If you want to make it look better, you can!

Enemy spaceships: Finally, the enemy spaceship, just a classy looking flying saucer.

Have a go hero

Why not try designing your own sprites? Make them look as cool as you like, cartoony or realistic, it's all up to you!

Making Level 1

This first level is going to be an easy level for the player. We are going to arrange our sprites into the scene. This is only our first level, so we will only include two asteroids in this level, adding more in later levels as the game goes on.

In the previous screenshot, you can see the level put together with two asteroids. After I did this, I duplicated the Big Asteroid actor in the Inspector, renamed it Small Asteroid and sized it down by half. So instead of 50 x 50 px, the Small Asteroid is 25 x 25 px. I created these Small Asteroid actors because when you shoot the Big Asteroids they will spawn three smaller asteroids like the original game. Cool huh?

1. Now, we are going to create a score actor. So, create a new actor and name it **Score**, open it up and change the **Width** to 100 and **Height** to 20.

2. Go back to the level editor, click the **Attributes** tab and click the + button to create a new attribute. When the selector comes up, choose **Integer**, and rename it to Score.

3. Now, go back to the **Actors** tab and double-click the **Score** actor, so we can add in some behaviors.

4. Add a **Display Text** behavior, and click the **e** beside the textbox, then click the down arrow to expand the **Expression Editor** and click **Game** and then **Score**, or you can even type in game.Score, and then click the green arrow to accept the changes. Change the size to 15, and keep the color white.

5. Now, we have to change the alpha of the actor, but we are going to hide it when the game starts to make it easier to arrange in the level editor.

6. All we have to do is drag in a **Change Attribute** behavior, change the **self.Color.Alpha** to 0.

7. Test the level to make sure it works and disappears when you play. If not, go back to double-check the behaviors and see if you typed everything in properly.

8. Now, we have to edit the asteroids. Double-click the **Big Asteroid**, so we can edit it. Add in a **Rotate** behavior and set the **Speed** to random(-50,50), so this will make the asteroids rotate at different speeds. The negative number will make it rotate counter-clockwise and the positive number will make it rotate clockwise.

9. Now, add in a **Move** behavior, and change the **Direction** to random(0,360), then change the **Speed** to random(5,50). This will make the asteroid move in a random direction from 0 to 360 degrees, and then the speed will make it move slow or fast.

What did we do? Just to recap, we added custom behaviors to randomize the movement of these asteroids; we varied the rotation, the speed, and the direction they move in with simple behaviors.

Time for action – player collisions

Now, we have to add in the collisions and explosions.

1. Let's edit our player. Double-click the **Player** actor in the **Inspector**. Add a rule, change it to **Actor receives event | overlaps or collides | with actor of type | Big Asteroid**. Now, add two **Particles** behaviors, on the particle event (this is going to be the shrapnel) and change the following settings:

- ◆ **Spawn Rate**:
  - ❑ **Number of Particles**: 20
  - ❑ **Particles Startup Time**: 1
  - ❑ **Particle Lifetime**: 2
- ◆ **Velocity/Position**:
  - ❑ **Direction**: random(0,360)
  - ❑ **Speed**: random(20,100)
- ◆ **Size**:
  - ❑ **Size**: random(2,15)
- ◆ **Color**:
  - ❑ **White Color Does not Change**
- ◆ **Rotation**:
  - ❑ **Angular Velocity**: 50

- **Image**:

    ❏ Draw an image for the flying shrapnel.

The previous image is the one I drew. It has really sharp-jagged edges that make it look like it blew apart!

2. Now, for the second **Particle Event**, change the following settings:

- **Spawn Rate**:
    ❏ **Number of Particles**: 4
    ❏ **Particles Startup Time**: 0
    ❏ **Particle Lifetime**: 2

- **Velocity/Position**:
    ❏ **Direction**: 0
    ❏ **Speed**: 0

- **Size**:
    ❏ **Size**: 15 | **Size changes to** | **Size Transiton**
        ❏ **Target Size**: 100
        ❏ **Duration**: 0.3 **seconds**

- **Color**:
    ❏ **Color: Banana**
    ❏ **Blending: Additive**
    ❏ **Color Transiton | Target Color: Black**
    ❏ **Duration**: 1 **second**

- ◆ **Rotation:**
    - ❑ **Angular Velocity:** 50
- ◆ **Image:**

Draw or download an explosion image, there are so many explosion sprites on the Web, just make sure it has a black background.

3. That looks pretty cool! Now, we have to destroy the ship and reset the level. Click the **Attributes** tab in the **Inspector**. Now, click the + button, choose a **Boolean** attribute and name it Dead?, or something similar.

4. Go back to editing the **Player** actor. Now, add a **Change Attribute** behavior and change it to **game.Dead?** | **To:** | **true**.

5. Now, add another rule and change it to **Attribute** | **game.Dead?** | **is** | **true**. Add a timer and change it to **Every** 1 **second**, then add a **Destroy** behavior.

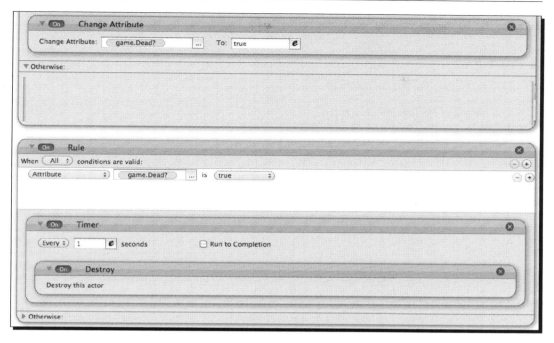

6. Next go back to the level editor and double-click the background image to edit it.

7. Create a rule and change it to **Attribute | game.Dead? | is | true**; add a **Timer** and change it to **Every** 3 **seconds**, then add a **Reset Scene** behavior to the Timer, and change its attribute to **Change Attribute: | game.Dead? | To: | false**, as shown in the previous screenshot.

You have to be very careful about the previous one. The **Change Attribute** behavior **MUST BE** below the **Reset Scene** behavior. This way the level will reset before the attribute is changed, if it was the other way around the attribute would be changed, and the level wouldn't reset because the Rule is no longer true.

Test it to make sure it works, if not, go back and check all your behaviors to make sure everything was typed in right.

What just happened?

With some more complex behaviors, we were able to call some behaviors after a collision; we changed an attribute on a collision, created some awesome-looking particle effects, and reset the level all due to that one collision.

Time for action – making the asteroids go kaboom!

Now, we are going to do the behaviors for the asteroids, such that, when you shoot at them, they break into three smaller asteroids. First off, you have to create the laser image.

1. Double-click our **Level 1**, so we can edit it. Now, import that image into our game and create a new actor from it and name it `Laser`.

2. Double-click the **Big Asteroid** actor, so we can edit it. Create a new rule and name it `Destroy` or something easy to remember.

3. Change the rule settings to **Actor Receives Event | overlaps or collides | with Actor of type | Laser**. Now, add in three **Spawn Actor** behaviors, changing the **Actor** setting for each one to **Small Asteroid**, then drag in a **Destroy** behavior, as shown in the following screenshot:

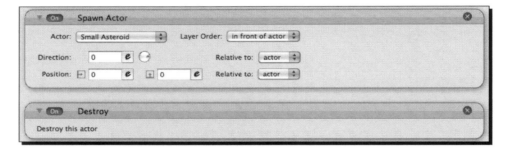

4. Now, we have to edit the **Small Asteroid** actor, but before we go to edit it, copy the two **Rotate** and **Move** behaviors from the **Big Asteroid**, so we can paste them into the **Small Asteroid** just to save some time.

You can save even more time by saving that behavior as a custom behavior. Don't know how? In the **Library**, click the **Custom** tab, and drag your behavior into the custom box.

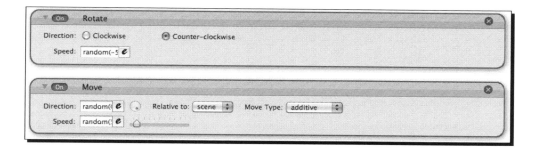

5. Double-click the **Small Asteroid** and paste these behaviors in. Now, we have to add in a new rule, change it to **Actor Receives Event | overlaps or collides | with Actor of type | Laser**, then add in a **Destroy** behavior.

6. Now, we have to work on the laser. Double-click to edit it; change the **Blending mode** to **Additive**, to give it a glowy look.

7. We now have to add in a few rules, one for the **Big Asteroid**, and another for the **Small Asteroid**. Create a rule and let's start with the **Big Asteroid**, change it to **Actor receives event | overlaps or collides | with actor of type | Big Asteroid.**

8. Add in a **Destroy** behavior, then drag in a **Change Attribute** behavior. Change the attribute from **game.Score** to **game.Score + 10**. This will add 10 points to the score each time you hit the asteroid. Do the same for the **Small Asteroid**.

What just happened?

We were able to set up a simple scoring system that will be used throughout each level, no need to set up separate **Score** attributes per level. This is a global attribute that can be accessed throughout the game. Later, we are going to look at uploading our score to Game Center.

Time for action – creating the sound effects! (pew pew kaboom)

Ok, we need to add a little more juice to this game, sound effects! No game is complete without them! Let's start off with playing a song at the beginning of our game, right at the splash screens. Create a song in **GarageBand**, if you have it, because then you can use it royalty-free, but if you can't, download some indie music, or royalty-free sound effects/songs (keep in mind you only have to do this, if you are planning on making money; if you aren't going to make money, you can use any song you want). I'm going to use something retro, "**The Final Countdown**".

1. When you are importing the song, GameSalad will ask you whether you want to import the song as a **music file** or a **sound file**. Of course, for this, we will select **music file**. Let's go to our first level, which is our splash screen, and double-click the actor that is displaying your logo. Then simply drag the song into the behaviors area. When you test your game, the music will start playing.

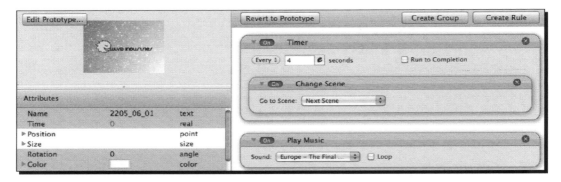

2. Now, let's add in the sounds for the asteroids being destroyed. Let's go to our **Inspector** and double-click the **Big Asteroid** actor. Download an explosion sound and import it into GameSalad. Once you have done that, drag the sound effect into the **Destroy** rule. Alternatively, you can drag in a **Play Sound** behavior then select the sound effect you want, but I find it quicker just to drag the sound effect into the rule you want.

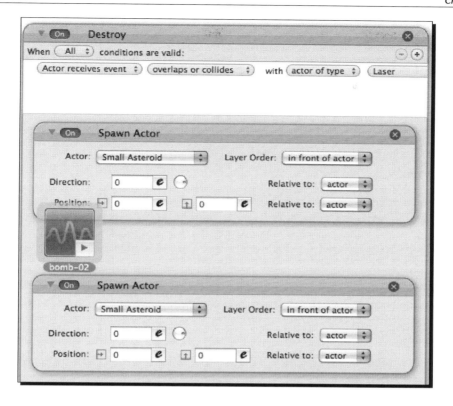

3. Do the same for the **Small Asteroid**.

4. Now, for the **Player**, double-click it. Download a different explosion sound effect, something destructive and sounds like there is shrapnel flying around. We want this to be somewhat realistic right? If you don't want to, you can always set a car horn sound effect for the player exploding, that will make the player laugh. Do whatever you want, make it your awesome masterpiece.

5. Where was I? Oh yes... the player dying. Ok, so all we have to do is drag our sound effect into the **Die** rule and watch, or should I say listen to the magic! Also, if you want, you can play a failed sound effect to find out where you put the rule that will reset the level after the player dies; in our case, we put it in the **Background** actor. Drag in the sound, or music file that you want in the **Timer** within the **Rule**, this will play the sound just before the level resets.

Have a go hero

Have a try! Find your own sound effects and music files for these rules, make them as realistic or hilarious as you like! Whatever you feel would be most appealing to the player.

Creating spaceship movement

Now, we are going to focus on the movement of our player. There are a few ways that we could use to set up the controls, we could do touch or tilt controls, but we are going to use touch controls for rotating, and tilt controls for accelerating. Let's start with the acceleration.

Time for action – player acceleration

Now for the fun bit, and the most critical... the player movement!

1. Double-click the **Player** actor to edit it. Click the **Create Group** button, and name it Movement. Make sure **Group** is selected; when it is, you can see a blue outline around it. If it isn't, select it. Now, click the **Create Rule** button and you should see a new rule within your group. If not, simply drag the new rule into it.

2. Rename the rule to Acceleration and change the settings to: **Attribute | game. Accelerometer.X | > | 0.5**. This says that when the accelerometer on the X axis is greater than 0.5g, which means the device is in landscape and tilted forward.

3. Now, add an **Acceleration** behavior, change the **Direction** to 90, and leave **Acceleration** at 100. Now would be a good time to limit the speed the player can get to, in the actors attributes box; expand the **Motion** roll out, change the **Max Speed** to 200, and check the **Apply Max Speed** box.

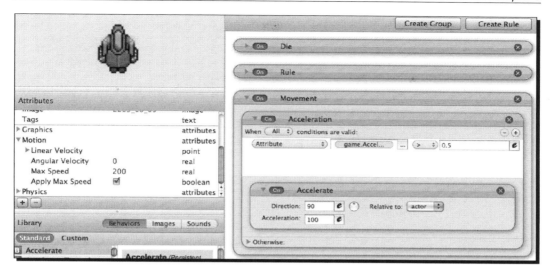

What just happened?

We were able to utilize the power of GameSalad and the iPhone to use the device's accelerometer to accelerate our player in one simple rule! GameSalad just keeps getting easier!

Time for action – player rotation buttons

Now, we need to go back to the **Scene Editor**. In the **Inspector**, we need to create two new actors; name one **Left** and the other **Right**. These will be the buttons that will rotate our player.

I used an image of a joystick thumb pad for my buttons in the game, but you can use any image you like.

1. In the **Attributes** tab, create a new attribute, select **Integer**, and then name it Rotation. Now, go back to the **Actors** tab and double-click our **Left** actor.

2. Change the **Width** and **Height** to 50, and then in the **Color** roll-out change the **Alpha** to something barely visible, so .5 or less would be perfect. Just make sure the player can see it, as shown in the following screenshot:

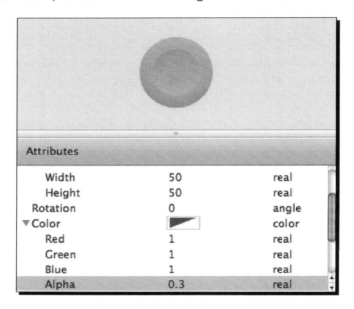

3. Now, let's create a new rule, and name it Pressed, then change the rule settings to **Actor Receives Event | touch | is | pressed**.

4. Then add a **Change Attribute** behavior into the rule, and change its settings to: **Change Attribute: | game.Rotation | To: | 1**.

5. Expand the **Otherwise** roll-out and copy the **Change Attribute** behavior in there and change it to 0 instead of 1.

6. Now, go to the **Right** actor and do the same. Change its **Width** and **Height** to 50, the **Alpha** to something less then .5 and repeat the rule, name it Pressed, then change the rule settings to **Actor Receives Event | touch | is | pressed**.

7. Then add a **Change Attribute** behavior into the rule, and change its settings to: **Change Attribute: | game.Rotation | To: | 2**.

8. Expand the **Otherwise** roll-out and copy the **Change Attribute** behavior in it, and change it to 0 instead of 2.

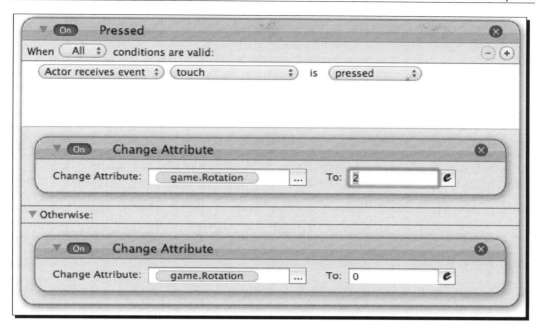

What just happened?

In this rule, when the player touches the button it will change the **Rotation** attribute to 1, then the **Otherwise** roll-out will change it to 0 when the player isn't touching it. Thus, it stops the actor from rotating once the player isn't touching the button.

Time for action – rotating the player

Now, we have to go back and edit the **Player** actor. Double-click it in the **Inspector**, so we can make some changes.

1. Create two rules in our **Player** actor, name them Left and Right and drag them into our **Movement** group. We are putting all our movement behaviors into one group to make things a lot less cluttered, because, trust me, when you start making a game with numerous complex behaviors, things can get a little messy. So putting all relevant behaviors into one group is just a smart thing to do.

2. Change the **Left** rule to **Attribute | game.Rotation | = | 1**

3. Then drag in a **Rotate** behavior, change it to **Counter-clockwise** and leave the **Speed** at 90.

4. Do the same for the **Right** rule:

    ❑ **Attribute | game.Rotation | = | 2**

    ❑ **Rotate** behavior **Clockwise Speed** 90

Run your level to see if it works.

Sure enough it does!

Now, I want to make the UI look a little better, I want a nicer-looking HUD so I'm going to design one.

Now, let's import that into GameSalad to see how it looks...

It looks pretty good! I added an **Additive** blending option to it to make the green outlines glow like a computer screen. Awesome!

By now, you must love GameSalad because it is easy to use. Plus, it's so powerful! We haven't even gotten into some of the really complex things, but GameSalad makes all that so simple!

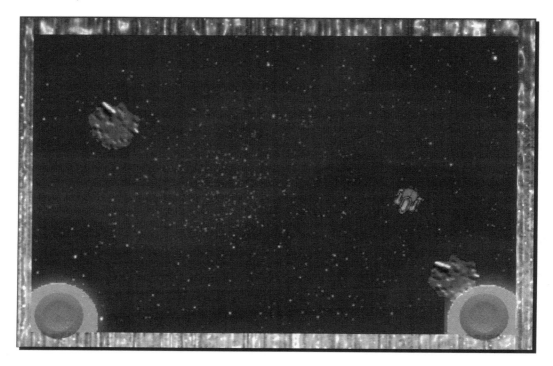

In the previous screenshot, as you can see, I am actually testing the game on my device.

In the next chapter, we are going to look at testing for a particular using the GameSalad Viewer, as well as actually deploying the game onto your device. We are also going to look at wrapping the actors around the screen (when the actor reaches the edge of the screen it will wrap around to the opposite end of the screen, so it doesn't disappear), shooting your lasers, particle boosters to make the game look better, Game Center leaderboards, and more levels including ones with alien ships! Are you excited to get into it? Me too! Let's take a look at what it's going to look like first, just to whet your appetite...

Ooh! It's giving me the chills, it looks so much fun! Are you eager to get to it now? Well, go ahead! Turn to the next chapter and I'll see you there!

Pop quiz

1. How do you detect forward tilt acceleration?

    a. Add a **Move** behavior with a direction of **game.Accelerometer.X**

    b. Create a rule that has an attribute of **game.Accelerometer.X**

    c. All of the above

    d. None of the above

2. What does the change in the **Move** behavior's **Direction** to Random(0,50) and **Speed** to Random(5,50) do?

    a. Moves the actor at a random direction and speed

    b. Wraps the actor around the screen

    c. Shoots particles at a random speed

    d. None of the above

3. How do you spawn more than one actor?

    a. Drag a **Spawn Actor** behaviors and select **Number** then specify the number

    b. Drag a **Spawn Actor** behavior per number of actors you want to spawn

    c. You can't, only one actor can be spawned at one time

    d. None of the above

Summary

In this chapter, we started to create a good-looking game, we designed all the sprites to look really cool, then we started making some enemies (the asteroids). We added some zest into our "salad" by adding some sound effects, music, splash screens, and then to top it off, we looked at how to create some realistic spaceship movements.

7
Space Defender Part 2

The video game industry both for the consoles and the mobile platforms is massive and to be honest, who wouldn't want to be a part of it? Traditionally to make a good game you need huge knowledge and programming knowhow, and let's not forget about the physics you need to know, and so on. By the end of this chapter, you will know how to create your own masterpiece. With the power of GameSalad, anyone can create amazing games, and the game we have been making is a fun, and somewhat complex game to create.

So why wait any longer? I'm sure you want to finish reading what I have to say and learn even more, so let's see what we are going to do in this chapter:

- ◆ Wrapping actors around the level
- ◆ Giving your player some firepower
- ◆ Game Center Leaderboards
- ◆ Installing the GameSalad Viewer on your device
- ◆ Testing the game on your device

We are going to polish this game up, good enough to sell! Let's get to it, shall we? This is going to be a lot of fun.

Level Wrapping

Open up your game project, and let's edit the first playable level, **Level 1**. If you click the **Preview** button and watch, the asteroids just fly off the screen. That's no fun, is it? No way! So we are going to wrap the actors around the level. In other words, when an actor reaches the edge of the screen, it will wrap or teleport to the opposite side of the screen.

Ok, so very simply! In the **Inspector**, click the **Scene** tab and check the **Wrap X/Wrap Y**. Simple right?

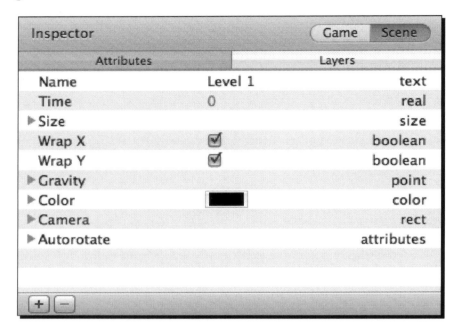

Creating more levels

Now, we have to check off the wrapping for all the playable levels, speaking of which, we have to make a few more levels. Go back to the project **Home** screen and click *Option* and select **Level 1** and duplicate it five or more times. For each level, we are going to add more hazards. So, it will be as shown:

- ◆ Level 1: 2 Asteroids
- ◆ Level 2: 4 Asteroids
- ◆ Level 3: 6 Asteroids
- ◆ Level 4: 6 Asteroids + 1 Alien spaceship
- ◆ Level 5: 6 Asteroids + 2 Alien spaceships
- ◆ Level 6: 6 Asteroids + 3 Alien spaceships

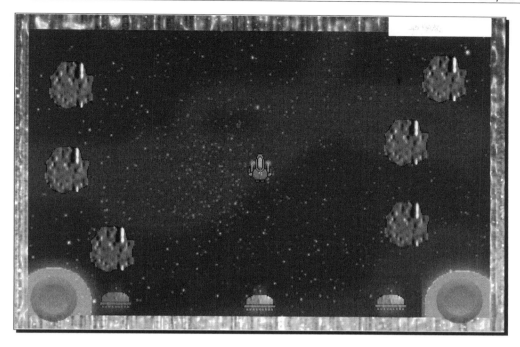

Arrange all the actors in each level. Don't place them too close to the player you don't want the player to start the level and get killed right away. See the previous screenshot for a good placement.

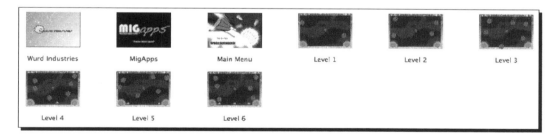

With two clicks, we were able to wrap the actors around the level. So, when the actor reaches the edge of the level, it will appear on the opposite edge of the level. Then we added more levels and arranged more actors, as shown in the earlier chapters. So, give it a try! Create your own copies of the levels and arrange them as you please. Just remember while you are arranging everything to make sure that as soon as the level starts, your player isn't going to get nailed by an asteroid. Place the asteroids and alien ships far away from the player.

Giving your player some firepower

For this section, we are going to look at making our player shoot. This will involve various different behaviors. We will be creating this feature with the help of the following steps:

1. Player taps

2. Player actor detects touch

3. Spawn Laser actor at player actor

4. Laser actor starts moving forward

It sounds daunting but don't worry, it certainly isn't! Let's dive right into it!

Time for action – making our player shoot

We need our player to shoot, or this game would not only be boring but highly unfair because you couldn't fight back!

1. Go back to our **Player** actor as we are going to edit it a little bit more. Create a new rule and name it `Shooting` and change it to **Actor Receives Event touch is outside**. By doing this, we don't have to set up a separate button to shoot. All the player has to do is tap outside of the **Player** actor, anywhere on the screen.

2. Now, add in a **Spawn Actor** behavior, change the actor to **Laser**, click the **e** and change it to **self.Rotation**.

3. Now, beside **Direction**, there is a drop-down box that says **Relative to:**, change it to **scene**.

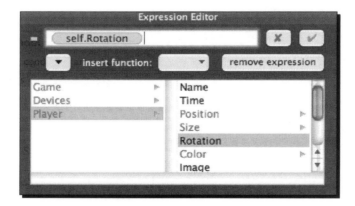

4. This will spawn the laser in the direction of the player. This is necessary and you will see why.

5. Now, we have to edit **Laser**. Double-click it so we can edit it. Create a new group and name it `Movement`. Add a **Move** behavior, changing the settings to the following:

- ❑ **Direction:** 90
- ❑ **Speed:** 100
- ❑ **Relative to: actor**

6. Test it out to see if it works. If it doesn't, take a look at the images, the previous and the following one; both of these behaviors are in our **Player** actors. Look for this **Movement** group, and the **Shooting** rule.

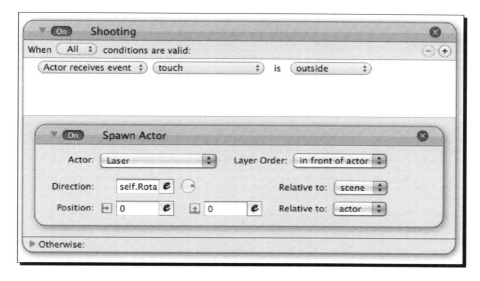

7. The previous screenshot is of the **Shooting** rule. If yours didn't work, check with it to make sure all the parameters were filled in correctly.

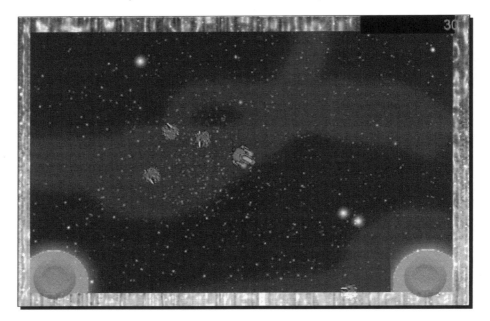

8. It works! And it works pretty well too, but I don't really like the fact that when the laser flies off the screen it just keeps going and going until it hits something. Sometimes there may be nothing for the laser to hit.

9. Ok, let's go back to the **Laser** actor, add in a **Timer** behavior and change it to **Every** 2 **Seconds**, then add in a **Destroy** behavior.

10. Just one more thing, let's add some thruster particles. Open up our **Player** actor, expand the **Movement** group and in the **Acceleration** rule, add in a **Particles** behavior with the following settings:

- ◆ **Spawn Rate** Tab:
    - ❑ **Number of Particles**: 100
    - ❑ **Particle Startup Time**: 2
    - ❑ **Particle Lifetime**: 0.5

- ◆ **Velocity/Position** Tab:
  - ❑ **Emitter Offset:** 0 **for both**
  - ❑ **Direction:** 0
  - ❑ **Speed:** 0
- ◆ **Size** Tab:
  - ❑ **Size:** 0 | **Size Changes To** | **Size Transition box:**
    - ❑ **Target Size:** 0
    - ❑ **Duration:** 0.3
- ◆ **Color** Tab:
  - ❑ **Color:** Turquoise
  - ❑ **Color changes to**
  - ❑ **Blending: Additive**
  - ❑ **Color Transition box:** | **Target Color:** Aqua
  - ❑ **Duration:** 1 **second**
- ◆ **Rotation** tab:
  - ❑ **Initial Rotation:** 0
  - ❑ **Angular Velocity:** 100

What just happened?

We let our player shoot; it kind of gives the game a little more sport, right? Then we spiced the game up a little more by adding in cool thruster particles!

Have a go hero

In a few clicks, we were able to add some weaponry to our player, very simply too. Why not try adding some more effects? For example, instead of a laser why not try making a rocket with smoke flying from it, and make those rockets heat-seeking! That would be cool.

Bringing our aliens to life

In this section, we are going to make our aliens come to life. We are going to make them shoot, and circle around the level. Then, we are going to add some particle effects to the rockets they shoot. So, what we have to do is edit the alien spacecrafts that will be circling around our level in the later levels. If you haven't already, create a new actor from the alien image that was provided for this book, or you can create your own. Now, we are going to start placing them in our levels, I added the first alien spacecraft in the fourth level, so let's go to that level and edit it. First, we will look at making them shoot!

Time for action – making the aliens shoot

1. We need to create a new rocket actor for our alien to shoot. Create a new actor and name it `Rocket`, and either design an image for it, or you can use the one that was provided for you in this book. We will come back to that actor later.

2. Then we need to create a new attribute. Click the **Attribute** tab and click the **+** button twice, make them **Integers**, and name them `Player X`/`Player Y`.

3. Next, in the **Inspector**, double-click our **Alien Craft** actor, so we can breathe life into it. Add in a **Move** behavior and change the settings to the following:

   □ **Direction:** `random(0,360)`

   □ **Speed:** `15`

   Leave everything else the way it is.

4. Now, let's add a **Timer** behavior, and change it to **Every** `random(2,10)`

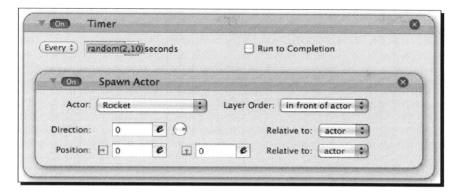

5. Then, add a **Spawn Actor** behavior to the **Timer** behavior and change the actor to `Rocket`.

6. Next go back to the **Inspector**, so we can edit the **Rocket**. Add in a **Timer** actor and change it to **For: 2 seconds**.

7. Then add a **Rotate to Position** and change it to the following settings:

   ❑ **Position:** → game.Player X ↑ game.Player Y

   ❑ **Offset Angle:** 270

   ❑ **Speed:** 90

8. One more thing, inside the **Rocket** actor, we have to add an **Accelerate** behavior. Change the **Direction** to 90 and the **Acceleration** to 100.

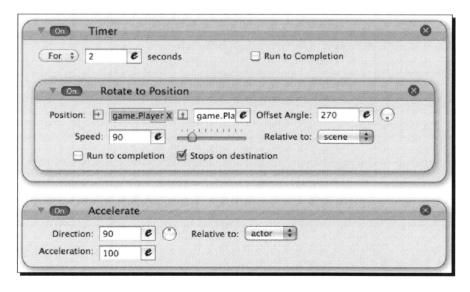

9. Finally, we have to employ those two blank player attributes that we created, that is, the X and Y ones. Double-click our **Player** actor and add two **Change Attribute** behaviors, set them to:

- ❑ **Change Attribute:** | game.Player X: | To | self.Position.X
- ❑ **Change Attribute:** | game.Player Y: | To | self.Position.Y

Test it out to see if it works, wait for the ship to start shooting, and just as you would expect, the rocket should come out of the ship and rotate towards you. Fantastic!

What just happened?

In just a few simple steps, we were able to create our aliens, and make them shoot at our player! Not only that but we made the rockets heat-seeking too!

Time for action – creating particle effects for the rockets

Now, we are going to spruce those rockets up with some particle effects:

1. Go back to our **Rocket** actor so we can add a particle behavior. Add it in and change the settings to:

- ◆ **Spawn Rate** Tab:
    - ❑ **Number of Particles:** 50
    - ❑ **Particle Startup Time:** 2
    - ❑ **Particle Lifetime:** 1

- ◆ **Velocity/Position** Tab:
    - ❑ **Emitter Offset** (both of them): 0
    - ❑ **Direction:** 0
    - ❑ **Speed:** 0

- ◆ **Size** Tab:
    - ❑ **Size:** 2 | **Size Changes To** | **Size Transition:**
        - ❑ **Target Size:** 10
        - ❑ **Duration:** 1

- **Color** Tab:
  - ❑ **Color**: `Tangerine`
  - ❑ **Color Changes To**
  - ❑ **Blending**: `Additive`
  - ❑ **Color Transition**: | **Target Color**: `Iron`
  - ❑ **Duration**: `0.5` **seconds**
- **Rotation** Tab:
  - ❑ **Initial Rotation**: `0`
  - ❑ **Angular Velocity**: `40`
- **Image** Tab:
  - ❑ **Set Image To**: `Laser` (I used the same image as the laser and it looks awesome)

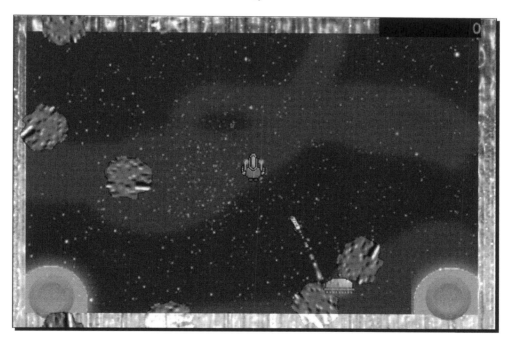

I think the effect looks pretty awesome!

What just happened?

We added some really cool-looking particle effects coming out of the rockets! Don't forget that I have only covered the flames coming out; why not try a shorter lifetime for the flame particles, and add in another particle behavior to simulate smoke? These are just small things, but in the long run your game will look better.

Time for action – rocket collision

Now that we have rockets flying around, we have to create the collisions. Because, as the famous saying goes "A rocket without collisions is like a rocket without collisions!". I'm just kidding, that's not a real saying!

1. Go back to the **Rocket** actor, add in a
    new group, and name it `Destroy Rocket`. Then add in a new rule, called `Ship`,
    and change its settings to **Actor receives event | overlaps or collides | with Actor
    of Type | Player.**

2. Next, simply drag in a **Destroy** behavior. One more thing, just so the rockets aren't
    flying around the level getting faster and faster, let's add in a **Timer** behavior; change
    it to 2 seconds. Then drag in a **Destroy** behavior, so that in two seconds if the rocket
    doesn't hit anything it will be destroyed. It makes sense, right?

3. Now we have to do the same with the **Player** actor. Go back to the level,
    double-click the **Player** actor in the **Inspector**, and change the settings to
    Actor receives event | overlaps or collides | with Actor of type : | Rocket.

4. Open up the **Die Big Asteroid** rule, and copy the **Shrapnel**, **Explosion**, **Play Sound**,
    and **Change Attribute** behaviors into this rule you just created. This way, when the
    rocket hits the player, he won't just disappear, there will be a nice explosion and
    some sound effects.

5. Then we have to detect the collisions of the player's laser with the alien spacecraft.
    Double-click the **Alien Craft** actor and add in a new rule and name it `Kill`, and
    change the settings to **Actor Receives event | overlaps or collides | with Actor
    of Type | Laser.**

    Then drag in a **Destroy** behavior.

What just happened?

We created some more enemies! And now, some of them shoot at you!

Ending the game

Wonderful! The game is almost done, but we have a few small additions to make; first off, we have to detect if the player has destroyed all the enemies and if so we have to move them on to the next level.

Time for action – detecting when all enemies are gone

For this section, we are going to create an attribute, the value of which will be reduced by 1 each time we destroy an enemy. Once all the enemies are destroyed it will take us to another level.

1. For this, we have to create a new game-wide attribute. So, go into your first playable level. In the **Inspector** with the **Game** button selected, click the **Attributes** tab, then click the **+** button to create a new attribute. Select the **Integer** option. Then click the **Choose** button and rename it to `Enemies Left`.

2. Go to the first level, **Level 1**, and double-click the **HUD** actor in the level, click the big lock button to edit this level's HUD only. Drag in a **Timer** attribute and set it to **For** 0.1 **second**.

3. Then drag in a **Change Attribute** behavior, and change it to **Change Attribute: | game.Enemies Left | To | 8**.

4. Two big asteroids create three small asteroids, so 2 + 6 = 8. So, this will change the **Enemies Left** attribute to 8 in the first fraction of a second of gameplay. Unfortunately, GameSalad doesn't have a behavior to detect the start of the level as in The Games Factory, but this will work.

5. Now, let's go back into the **Big Asteroid** actor (the main one in the **Inspector**, not the one in the levels because that just won't work), open the **Destroy** group that we created, and add in a **Change Attribute** behavior at the very top of the group. Change it to the following **Change Attribute**: | game.**Enemies Left** | **To:** | game.**Enemies Left -1**.

6. Do the same for the **Small Asteroid**, and the **Alien Craft** actor. Now, double-click the **HUD** actor again as we are going to add in a new rule. Click the **Create Rule** button, rename it to Next Level, and change it to **Attribute** | game.**Enemies Left** | = | 0.

7. Add in a **Timer** behavior, change it to **Every** 2 **seconds**.

8. Drag in a **Change Scene** and change it to Next Scene if you have to.

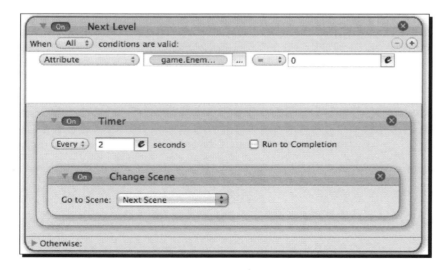

9. Test the level just to make sure it works. If it doesn't, just go back through the steps to make sure everything was filled out properly.

10. We now have to repeat the steps for the HUD for each level. So, to save some time, create a new group within the **HUD** actor, name it `Enemy Detection`, drag in all the behaviors into the group, then drag that group into the custom section of the **Behaviors**, as shown in the following screenshot:

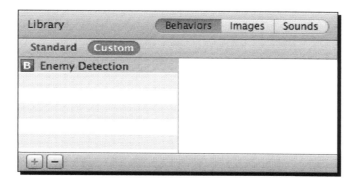

11. That will make things so much easier because when editing the rest of the levels, you don't have to keep creating all the behaviors each time. Now, let's go over the figures for all the levels:

Level	Number for Enemies in the level
1	8
2	16
3	24
4	25
5	26
6	27

12. Just go into each level, double-click the **HUD** actor, and drag in the custom **Enemy Detection** behavior, changing the **Enemies Left** value accordingly.

13. Test each level to make sure everything works.

What just happened?

We looked at a beginner's way to detect whether all enemies have been destroyed in the level. This is a preset attribute that we set at the beginning of each level, depending on the amount of enemies.

Time for action – creating Leaderboards

This section is going to be real fun! We are going to set up the scoring and Game Center Leaderboards. These will make the game much more enjoyable for players because they can compare with and challenge their friends.

1. Go to www.iTunesConnect.Apple.com to set up your leaderboards. If you have your app set up already, click on the app and then click the **Manage Game Center** button. Then click the **Set Up** button under the Leaderboard section.

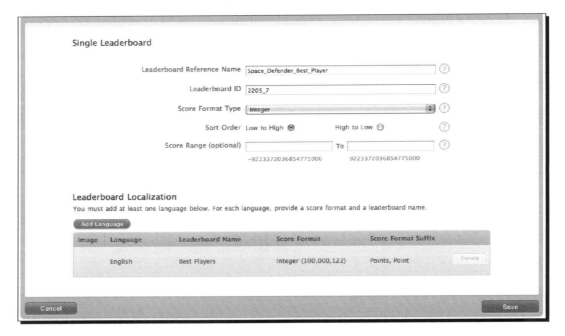

2. Fill it out as shown:

 - **Leaderboard Reference Name**: Space_Defender_Best_Player
 - **Leaderboard ID**: 2205_7 (this can be anything you want)
 - **Score Format Type**: Integer
 - **Sort Order**: Low to High

3. Then click the **Add Language** button to set up your language in the leaderboard. The more languages, the more it will appeal to international players.

4. Now, go back to GameSalad; add one more level and name it `Leaderboards`. This will be the very last level, so drag it to the end if you have to. Add in the **Background** actor and double-click it to edit it click the big lock button so we can edit this actor.

5. Drag in a **GameCenter – Post Score** behavior and change it to:

  ❑ **Post Attribute**: `game.Score`

  ❑ **Leaderboard ID**: `2205_7`

6. Add in a **Timer** behavior and change it to **Every** 5 **seconds**, then drag in a **Change Scene** behavior, and change it to the `Main Menu` level.

7. Now, go back to the **Main Menu**, *Option* + left-click the **Text Button** actor we have there in our scene; double-click the copy so we can edit it.

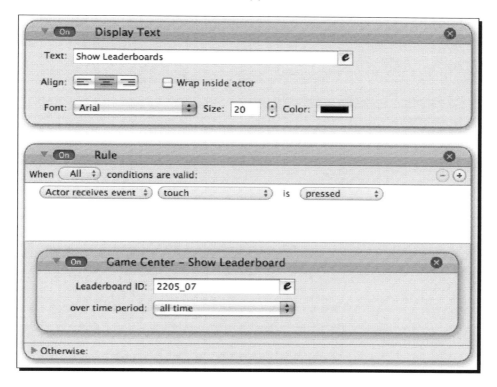

8. Change the **Display Text** behavior to Show Leaderboards, then delete the **Change Scene** behavior in the rule. Drag in a **Game Center – Show Leaderboard** behavior and change it to:

❑ **Leaderboard ID:** 2205_07

❑ **Over time period:** all time

That's it for the game! Now, it's kind of difficult to play your game without actually having it on the device, isn't it? Well, buckle up my friends because it's time!

Testing your game on your device

It is now time to talk about deploying your game to the device. This is great! It's important to see how your game runs on the device, because don't forget, your computer is way more powerful than the iPhone, so the performance will differ considerably.

Time for action – installing GS viewer on your device

First off, we are going to discuss the GameSalad viewer. The GameSalad viewer is a great way to test your game without having to publish your project, create provisioning profiles and go through the whole installation of the app every time.

1. First, we download the viewer. Go to www.GameSalad.com, scroll down to the bottom of the page and click **Download iOS Viewer**.

GameSalad	Games	Support	Community	About Us
Download Creator	Arcade	Getting Started	Forums	Press Center
Download iOS Viewer	Accelerator	Cookbook	Invite	Press Kit
Terms of Use	Success Stories	FAQs	Blog	Team Help Wanted
Privacy Policy		Report a Bug		Contact Support

2. This will download an Xcode project. Open it up because you have to edit the .PLIST under the **Bundle Identifier**. In my case, I had a provisioning profile that required a bundle identifier of com.wurdindustries.gs. If you don't know what I'm talking about, then turn to the Appendix and I've explained everything there.

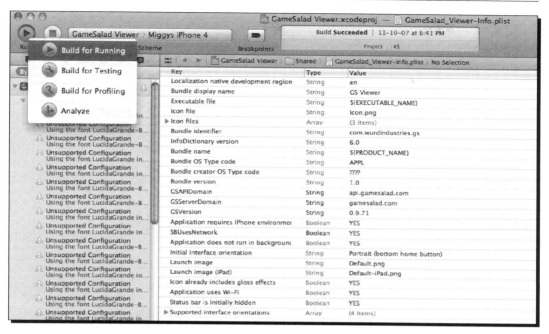

3.   Next plug in your iPhone or iPod Touch and click the **Run** button (see the previous screenshot), it will build the project and then deploy it to your device.

You can choose what you want to test your project on within Xcode (device or simulator). If you look at the previous screenshot, beside the **Run** and **Stop** button, you will see a box that says **GameSalad Viewer** (or whatever the name of your project is), beside that there is a drop-down box, which in the screenshot says **Miggy's iPhone 4**. If you click on this, a drop down box will appear showing your device, the iPhone Simulator and the iPad simulator.

4. Now, open it up on your device, and you will see a big GameSalad logo. If you are connected to Wi-Fi, it will say at the bottom **Connected to wifi Waiting for GameSalad Creator**. Now, if you go back to GameSalad, you will see a new button, **Preview on iPhone**.

5. Click that button and you will see GameSalad install on to your device and then you can play the game on your device!

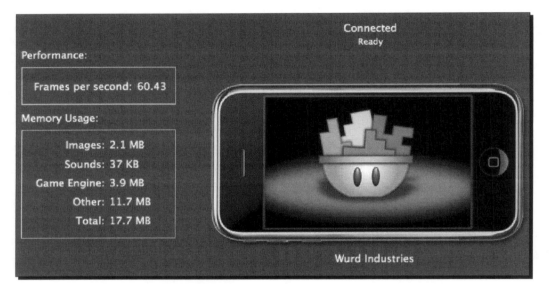

What just happened?

You learned how to install the GameSalad viewer, and to test your game on the device through the GameSalad simulator.

Have a go hero

Try adding in some more functionality, have a go at trying things such as charring the player when he explodes, disabling the player so he can't control it after he's dead, setting up leaderboards for each level, and other cool functionalities.

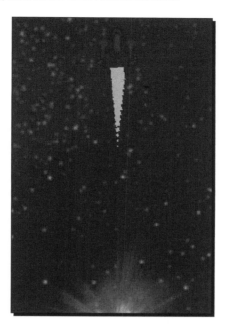

Pop quiz

1. How do you wrap actors around the screen?

   a. In the **Inspector** under **scene/attributes**, check off **Wrap X/Y**

   b. Create a rule that has a **Wrap** behavior

   c. Right-click the actor and check off the Wrap icon

   d. None of the above

2. What does **Leaderboard ID** do?

   a. It is an integer that differentiates your Leaderboard from every other app

   b. It is an integer that differentiates specific Leaderboards within your game

   c. It allows players to look up the Leaderboard online

   d. None of the above

3. What is the advantage of **Custom Behaviors**?

   a. Quick access between actors

   b. Saves loads of time in developing

   c. Helps you concentrate on other aspects of the game, not behavior

   d. All of the above

Summary

Did you enjoy it? I did! I thought this was a really fun exercise that bent the brain with nice complex behaviors, and really tested your skills. We aren't done yet though! We still have one more game to do! This one will be called Metal Mech and it will essentially be a game similar to the old Mech Warrior games, except 2D. This will have lots of AI that will have line of sights, and more. This one is going to be done with all 3D sprites, so it's going to look awesome! But, I'm sure you need a break. Go and have a nice tea or a coffee and we will get back to the awesome development that GameSalad allows us to do so easily.

8
Metal Mech Part 1

Well this is it! The final game that we are going to make. This one is going to be more complex, as it will have intelligent NPC's with a line of sight that will detect you and turn to shoot you, big levels with objectives, and more! This is not only going to be a fun game to play, but it's also going to be a super fun game to create! This game is going to be divided into four parts; we need to split it up, so we can take a break between the chapters. Remember the old MechWarrior games? Those were fun! I remember borrowing a copy of the second one and at the time the graphics were great, the gameplay was addictive and it was one of those games that everyone had to play, so we are going to create a "clone", maybe not quite the same but we will make it our own little masterpiece that once you are done reading this book you can expand on it, both story and game play! We are going to have a lot of fun in this section, so fasten your seat belts because it is going to be a wild ride!

Let's take a look at what we are going to cover in this chapter:

- Designing a good user interface
- Designing good, long levels with objectives
- Designing the characters
- Setting up line of sights for enemies

This is going to be a creative chapter, with lots of designing, both within our design software and within GameSalad. Now that we have an idea what we are going to be doing in this chapter, let's get to it.

Designing our interface!

First off, let's design our main menu, this is going to be a very good-looking game. I am going to use 3D Studio Max to create everything in the game, but you can use whatever you like.

The previous screenshot will be my main menu image; I'm just going to put it aside for now. We will import our images into GameSalad all at once. In the old Mech games, there was a very technical interface that gave you information on everything about your mech; it looked like an old computer was flashing a heads up display in front of you, lots of greens, numbers, and bars.

As you can see in the previous screenshot, there was a mini map or radar, a compass, and multiple health bars showing the condition of your mech. So, we are going to design something close to this. It doesn't have to be exact because this is honestly a really complex user interface (UI) and while we are creating a complex game, we don't want our UI to daunt the player. Our UI is going to be simpler; we can have a compass, a speedometer, health, and weapon energy bars. We can create the bars and numbers within GameSalad, so we don't have to worry about those just now, but let's design the base of the UI.

The following screenshot shows a design of a basic UI:

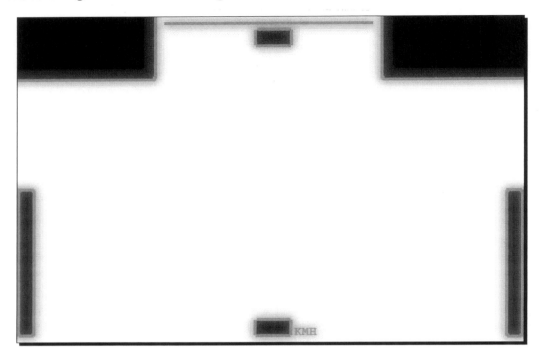

It's a simple UI, but it will show all the information we need to know—the score, the direction you are going, your health, weapon heat, and your speed. Plus, there is a slight glow effect on this image, so when we import it into GameSalad, we can add an **Additive** blending effect to make it glow even more. Let's continue. One big thing that I've learned when creating a game is that you **HAVE** to explain to the player how to play, describe the controls, how the HUD works, and so on. This is imperative because if the person doesn't know how to play, all your hard work goes down the drain with frustrated players who have to learn the controls themselves. So a good thing to do is create a *loading* screen that will explain everything before the player dives into the game. So, let's do that. Create a nice loading screen that will show up between the main menu and the first level.

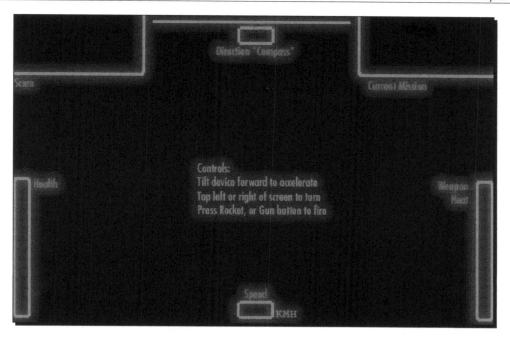

Of course we are going to add in the buttons and even an ammo counter for the bullets and the rockets, which will be in the score box at the upper-left corner of screen as shown in the previous screenshot. These buttons have to look the same as the rest of the HUD, as shown:

The following screenshot is the button to shoot your guns:

The following screenshot is the button to shoot rockets:

Designing good, long levels

Now, we have to be very creative here, as we have to design all the levels. Create them with objectives in mind, such as something like "The opposing team has invaded our fortress just on the other side of the forest, you must walk around the forest avoiding enemy patrols to infiltrate our base and take it back." For these levels, I am going to use 3D Studio Max, to keep with our 3D realism theme; rendering these images is taking a long time but I know they will look fantastic.

This will be our first level, and as you can see it looks great. This was rendered at 1200x1200px with high-resolution textures, 8 omni lights with full textures being rendered.

This image took my HP Pavillion 3.0 GHz AMD Black 6 Core Processor with 12 GB of ram and 1GB video card (so in other words a super powerful computer) over a minute to render, but it looks great! When we import this image into our level we will create bounds around the level so the player cannot walk through the tree line. You can make your levels a lot longer, I just made these ones up quickly. It would be a good idea to make the level beatable within 5-10 minutes, so make it a big level, something double or even triple the size of our image here. Keep in mind that when we import this image into GameSalad it will automatically resize it because it will be "too big" to import, but all we have to do is simply resize it to the full size in the Scene Editor.

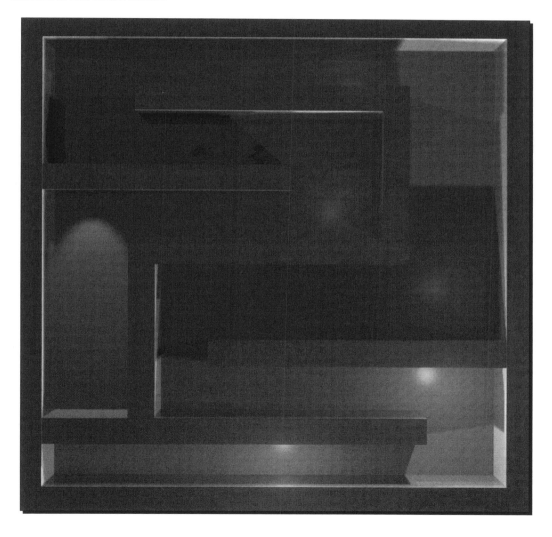

This image gives us an idea of how our indoor levels should look, don't forget it looks plain right now, but we are going to populate it with computers, and other mechs within GameSalad. Just some tips to remember when designing our levels:

♦ Make it look amazing, dramatic lighting, bump textures, realism to the full.

♦ Fill it up! Put lots of cool-looking scenery, objects, and other things that will add to the visual experience.

♦ Make lots of memorable moments in the level, things that will make the player say, "Wow, remember what happened when you get to the bridge? You haven't gotten there yet?! I'm not going to tell you what happens because you will be shocked!"

♦ It doesn't have to be "big", you can make a medium-sized level with lots of things to do in it that will drag out the gameplay time. Try to be original.

♦ In Mario games, some levels are very short, but there are secrets you can find that make the level take double or triple the time to finish.

Designing the characters!

As with the levels we have been designing, we want to make our characters look fantastic and realistic. So, again, I am using 3D Studio Max to create the Mech for our player, and then doing minor edits to it in Photoshop for the enemies, for different markings and such.

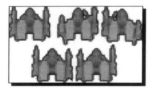

There they are, a stopped image, two walking, and two shooting animations. That's for our main character, so we need one for our enemy players.

They are essentially the same image, just slightly edited. Following is a screenshot of a turret:

The following is the screenshot for a projectile:

And finally, the following is the screenshot for particle effects:

Time for action – creating the Menu!

Ok, ok! Enough of the creating images. Let's take it into GameSalad!

1. Open up GameSalad and create a new project. We are going to name it `Metal Mech`.

2. We will start with the main menu, so rename the **Initial Scene** to `Main Menu`, and double-click it to bring up the **Scene Editor**. Import our menu image, and drag it into the scene.

3. Next, we have to create the buttons. In the **Inspector**, click the **+** button to create a new actor. Name it `Start Game Button` and double-click it so we can edit it.

4. Click the **Create Rule** button, change its settings to **Actor receives event | touch | is | pressed**.

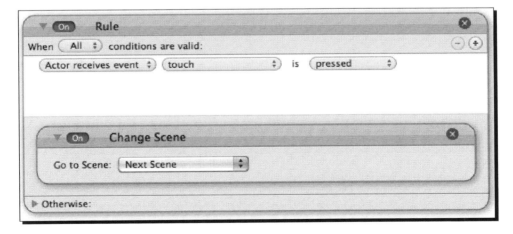

5. Drag in a **Change Scene** behavior and leave the setting at **Next Scene**. Now, we have to drag in a **Display Text** behavior, set the text to Play Game. Change the font to something cool like **Futura** and a size of 20 (or less) to make sure the text fits in the button image properly. Just to make it more appealing to the eyes, I made a nice metal button image for the button actor.

6. We next have to create a new level. This is going to be our loading/instructions screen. So, go back to the project **Home** screen, click the + button to create a new level. Rename it to Instructions. This is simply going to be an instructions screen telling the player how to play, what buttons do what, and what everything in the HUD does.

7. Import our instructions image into GameSalad, then create a new actor by either clicking the + button in the **Inspector** or, to make it easier, you can drag the image from the **Library** into the **Inspector**.

8. Double-click this actor, so we can add some behaviors into it. Next create a new rule and change its settings to **Actor receives event | touch | is | pressed**.

9. Then in that rule, drag in a **Change Scene** behavior and leave it at **Next Scene**. What this does is, when the player taps the screen, it will go to the next level, very simple.

What just happened?

We created our menu system; from our menu, the player is taken to an instruction screen to show the player how to play the game.

Time for action – creating the Objectives screen

Now, we are going to add a storyline screen. This is going to inform the player of his objectives. Create another level back in the project **Home** screen and name it `Level 1 - Objectives` and double-click it, so we can edit it.

1. This screen is going to be pretty cool, we are going to create a new game attribute. So click the **Attributes** tab with the **Game** button selected, then click the **+** button to create a new attribute. Select **text**, then click **OK**.

2. Rename your new attribute to `Player Name`, and change the text to something generic like `Commander`.

3. What we are going to do with this is, we are going to get the player to type in their name, and GameSalad will save it. So every time a character talks to you, they will use your name! Cool huh? Ok, let's continue. Create an awesome-looking image for the objective, something that looks similar to the following:

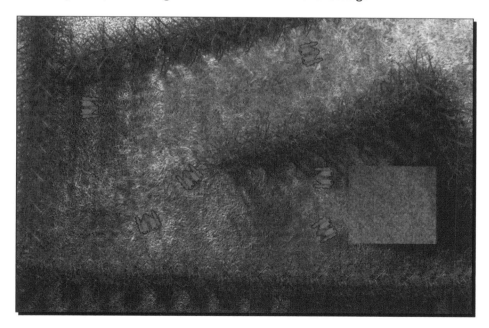

4. Import this image into GameSalad and create an actor out of it by dragging it from the **Library** to the **Inspector**, then drag it into the scene. Double-click it so we can edit it.

5. Simply add in a **Display Text** behavior, and click the italic **e** button beside the textbox. Now, click the black down arrow button, then click **Game | Player Name**.

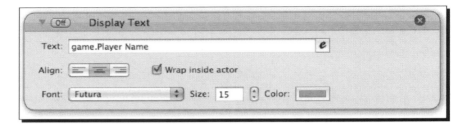

6. Change the **Font** to **Futura**, **Size** to `15`, and **Color** to **green**. Then we need to add in one more behavior; find **Keyboard Input** and drag it in. Change the settings to **Change Attribute: | game.Player Name | Keyboard Prompt | Type in your name**.

7. This will now bring up a keyboard and textbox. You can type in your name and it will display it on our image.

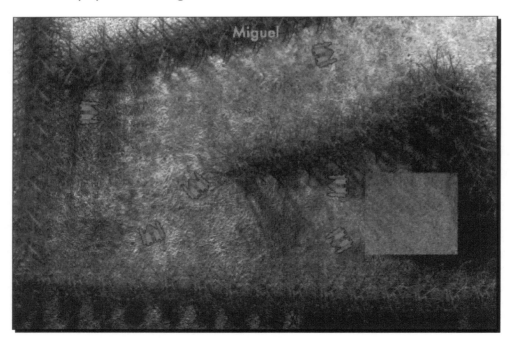

8. Pretty cool! Now, we have to continue the writing. For this, we have to create another actor, so create it in the **Inspector** and name it `Text`, then drag it into your level, and double-click it so we can add our text.

9. Add in a **Display Text** behavior and type in whatever you like. You can explain a little bit of the back story, and your objectives, then change the **Alpha** to `0`. If you don't remember how to do this, it's easy! You will find it in the **Color** drop-down in the **Attributes** box of the actor.

10. Now, create a new rule, and we are going to use the same **Tap to Begin** behavior. Change it to **Actor receives event | touch | is | pressed**.

11. Then drag in a **Change Scene** behavior and leave it at **Next Scene**.

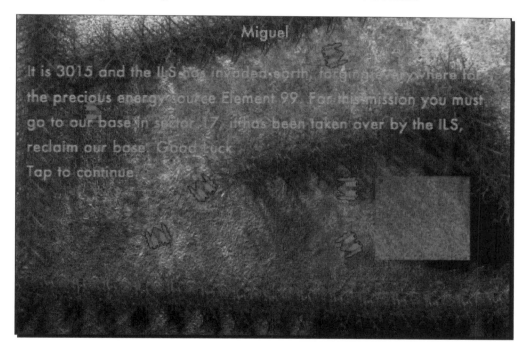

Now that that's done, we have to create our first level!

What just happened?

We created a really cool Objectives screen. This screen not only shows the objectives of the current level, but it also allows the player to type in their own name, and the level will use your name within the objectives! Cool!

Time for action – creating our first level!

1. This is going to be lots of fun! Go back to the project **Home** screen and click the **+** button, and name the new level `Level 1` accordingly.

2. Open up that new level and click the **Scene** button. Expand the **Size** roll-out and change the **Height** and **Width** to `1200` (the size of the image I created, but you can change it if yours is different).

3. Import the level image if you haven't already. Don't forget GameSalad will force you to resize the image upon importing, but once you make it an actor, you can resize it to however you like by dragging it into the scene.

4. Now, we have to populate this level. Import the character images, and create two new actors; name one `Player` and the second `Enemy`. We need to edit our **Player** actor, so let's open it up.

5. We are going to make two sets of movements for this actor, one for iOS and another for our computer, because we can't test an accelerometer on our Mac, unless you throw it, but I doubt it will register the "G"s and then you'll be out over a thousand dollars, so I don't recommend trying that option.

6. Click the **Create Group** button and rename the group to `Keyboard Movement`. Create a new rule and name it `Accelerate`, and change the settings to **Actor receives event | key | UP | is | down**

7. Now, add in a **Move** behavior, and change the settings to:
   - **Direction**: 90
   - **Speed**: 100
   - **Relative to: Actor**
   - **Move Type: additive**

8. Copy the new rule and rename it to `Reverse`. Change the rule settings to **Actor receives event | key | Down | is | down**, and change **Move** behavior **Direction** to `270`.

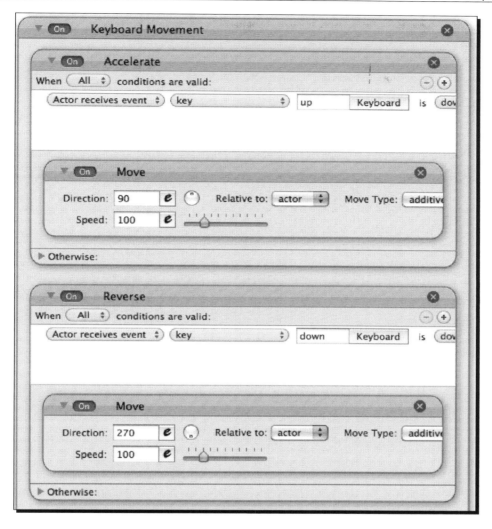

9. Create two new rules, name one Rotate Left and the other Rotate Right, and change the settings to **Actor receives event | key | left | is | down** (repeat for right key rule)

10. Add in two **Rotate** behaviors. For the **Left** rule, change the settings to:

- ❑ **Direction: Counter-Clockwise**
- ❑ **Speed:** 200

11. For the **Right** rule, change the settings to:

- ❑ **Direction: Clockwise**
- ❑ **Speed:** 200

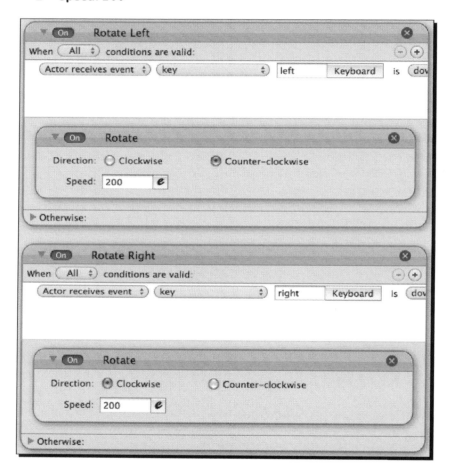

12. Finally, add in one more behavior, a **Control Camera** behavior. Test your level just to make sure all the controls are working alright, and don't forget to save your work.

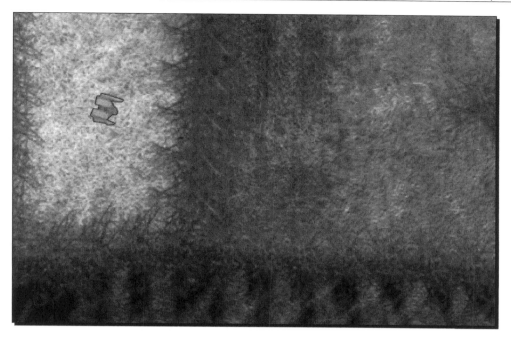

13. If your player isn't moving around, go back and make sure that you changed all the buttons to the appropriate key. I accidentally had two Rules with the **Up** key registering a move behavior in two different directions, that explains why he wasn't moving. At first, I thought he was just being a rebellious AI, but it was my mistake.

If you have a level with an on-top HUD layer that doesn't scroll, normally when you drag in a new actor, that new actor will automatically go onto the top layer, which causes unwanted results. What I do is move that HUD layer down below the main layer; that way, every new actor that you drag in will be on the main layer.

14. Ha-ha! Now go ahead, and pepper the level with baddies in groups of around three or four, the more clustered the better, because it will make the level a little longer.

15. Keep in mind that we have to leave some room between the enemies and the hedge, because we don't want our player to trigger an enemy's line of sight detector from across the hedge, this would not look good.

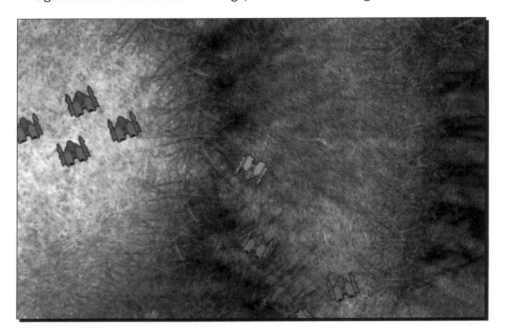

16. Next we need to create a way for the baddies to detect if our player is in range, so we need to create a new actor, name it `Detector`, and change its **Width** and **Height** to `200`; you can import a simple circle image for it.

17. Now, open up our **Enemy** actor (the main one in the inspector, not the one in the level), drag in a **Spawn Actor** behavior and select our **Detector** actor. This will take out a lot of time, instead of having to create one detector for each enemy. This simple behavior works with all of the enemies in the level.

18. Click the **Preview** button and you'll see one of these detectors for each bad guy.

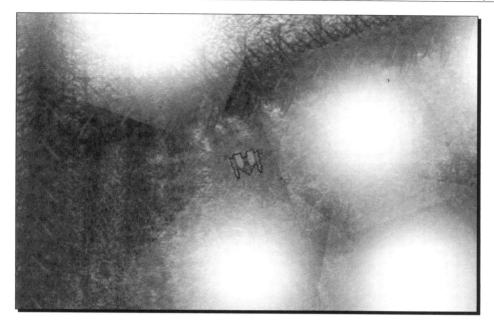

Oops, it looks like it's been snowing here. Go back to the **Detector** actor and set its **Alpha** to 0. That's better (because they will be gone)!

What just happened?

In a short period of time, we were able to create a really nice user interface, really awesome-looking characters, sweet levels, and even start designing the first level. We also learned how to input text into GameSalad, use that text to save an attribute, and use it throughout the game.

Have a go hero

Give this stuff a try! Everything that we have learned in this chapter, try doing it, but add your own twist to it, maybe instead of having the level as one big image, why not populate the level with actors for trees, bushes, and more? It's not difficult! I have complete faith in you my friend!

Wow! This game is looking pretty awesome, isn't it? We've only covered a little bit, just setting everything up for the game! Designing all the sprites, and menu images and then, we put it together in our game!

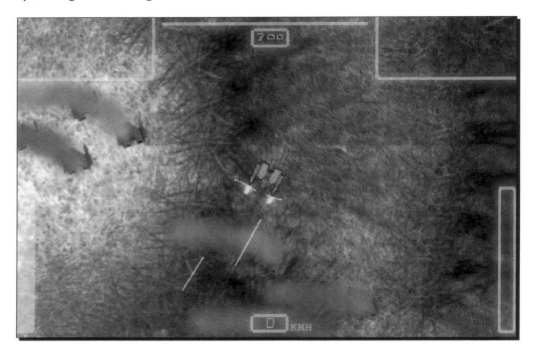

Expect the game to look something similar to the previous screenshot by the end of the next chapter. I can't wait! Can you? I don't see how! That's ok...

Go and take some rest. Pacing yourself is very important, especially when developing. The last thing you want to do is push yourself, then you get tired and make mistakes. As with all the other chapters, you can check out the GameSalad project files and all the images that were used.

Pop quiz

1. What blending mode for actors adds a glow-ish look?

    a. Subtractive

    b. Screen

    c. Opaque

    d. Multiply

2. How would you change the scene via a Finger Touch?

    a. Add in a rule that detects the tap then changes the scene

    b. Add in a behavior that finds and registers the touch, then changes the scene

    c. **game.Touch3 | is | true | Change Level to Next**

    d. None of the above

3. How do you bring up the keyboard for text input?

    a. GameSalad doesn't support keyboard input

    b. Add a textbox actor that can receive text

    c. Any behavior can bring up the keyboard

    d. None of the above

Summary

In this chapter, we started to put everything together. We designed the sprites and all the images, then took them into GameSalad, arranged everything, and even got our player moving around. We still have three more chapters to go! In the next chapter, we are going to add behaviors to make those detectors work, so that when you enter them, the enemy will start shooting at you. Then, we will look at your ability to retaliate; we are going to set up the player's weaponry, and more! There is still a fair amount to go for this game, but once it's done, it's going to be totally awesome!

9
Metal Mech Part 2

The last chapter was really fun, wasn't it? This game is going to be really cool! In this chapter, we are going to be adding a little more functionality and by the end, we are going to have a lot of the gameplay done. This chapter is going to be a lot of fun!

Let's take a look at what we are going to do in this chapter:

- ◆ Player shooting bullets and rockets
- ◆ Enemy detection with the line of sight
- ◆ Particle effects
- ◆ Player health

I'm just so excited to start this chapter, so let's dive right into it!

Making our player shoot!

What kind of game would this be if you weren't able to shoot back at our enemies? I don't think it would be very enjoyable. So, in this section, we are going to look at how to make our player shoot, and the first thing we have to do is create the images.

First, we are going to design our bullet image, a bullet image that will look like a blazing hot glowing projectile (which is totally wrong because the only time you can see bullets flying is when they are tracer rounds).

I drew a straight, white line, then copied the layer, added a Gaussian Blur with a .6 intensity, and colored it yellow, as shown in the following screenshot.

Time for action – creating bullet behaviors

Now that we have created the image for our bullets, we have to take it into GameSalad and start creating the bullet behaviors. This will involve movement, spawning, and more; so, let's get right into it.

1. Anyways, let's import that image into GameSalad. Create an actor and call it `Bullet` and drag in the bullet image (or directly drag the image from the **Library** to the **Actors** section to create an actor from that image). Double-click that actor so we can edit it. Under the **Graphics** roll-out, change the **Blending Mode** to `Additive`. Now, drag in a **Move** behavior and change the **Direction** to `90`, and the **Speed** to `1000`.

2. Next, go back into the scene editor, so we can edit our **Player** actor. Double-click it and under the **Keyboard Movement** group, create a new rule, name it `Shooting` and change the settings to **Actor receives event | key | space | is | down**.

3. Now, simply add in a **Timer** behavior, and change it to **Every** `0.2` **seconds**. Then, drag in two **Spawn Actor** behaviors. Change the settings of the first one to:

- **Actor**: `Bullet`
- **Direction**: `self.Rotation`
- **Position**: `-8 : 5`
- **Layer Order**: `in back of actor`
- **Direction Relative to**: `scene`

4. Change the settings of the second one to:

   - **Actor**: Bullet
   - **Direction**: self.Rotation
   - **Position**: 8 : 5
   - **Layer Order**: in back of actor
   - **Direction Relative to**: scene

5. If you're confused, take a look at the following screenshot to see if you did everything correctly.

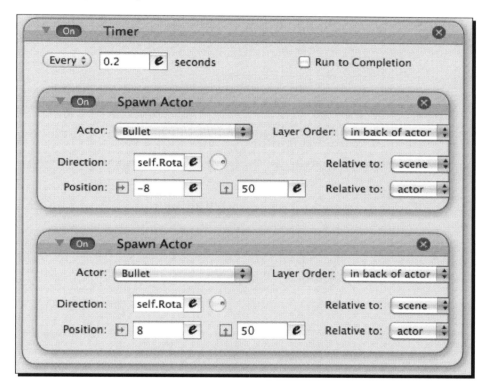

6. What this does is spawns a bullet at each of the barrels. Now, we are going to add in some cool-looking muzzle flashes.

7. This was done in a 3D program, but don't worry about the black outline; once we import it into GameSalad, we will use the blending mode to remove that.

8. Import it into GameSalad, then create a new actor and name it `Muzzle Flash`. Double-click it so we can edit it. Change the **Blending Mode** to `Additive`. Drag in a **Timer** behavior and change the timer to `0.1` **seconds**, then drag in a **Destroy** behavior.

9. Now, go back into the **Player** actor, so we can add in the muzzle flashes. All we have to do is simply clone the two **Spawn Actor** behaviors and change the clones to `Muzzle Flash`, and change the second position to `50` or more, whatever makes it look like it's coming right out of the barrel.

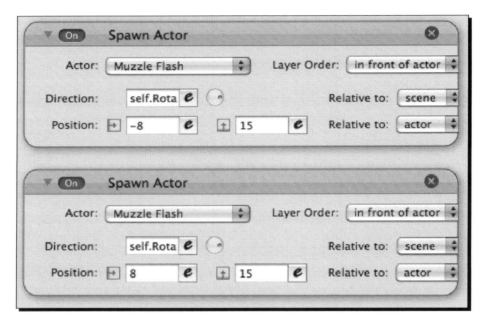

10. Take a look at the previous screenshot to see if everything is correct in your project. Now, let's save it and try it out.

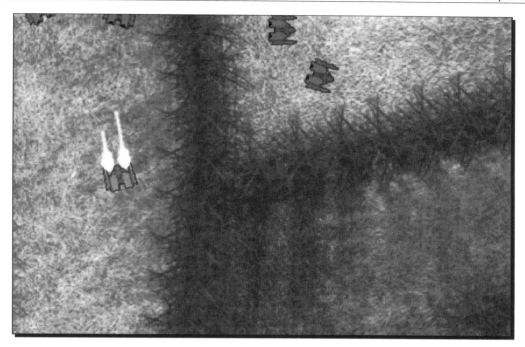

Voila! It looks pretty good, right? Now, we have to "program" the bullet collisions with the enemies.

What just happened?

In a few short moments, we were able to make our character shoot bullets in the direction our player faces and even spice it up with some muzzle flashes. A simple **Spawn Actor** behavior makes it quite easy to create many bullets! Unlike Xcode and programming our games, we don't have to set up an NSMutableArray similar to the following code:

(This code is here purely to show you the contrast between coding our game, and using GameSalad.)

```
//declare this in the header file
NSMutableArray *Array;
UIImageView *charShot;
BOOL shooting;
//code this in the main file
for(charShot in Array) {
  CGPoint newCenter = charShot.center;
  newCenter.x = newCenter.x + 25;
  charShot.center = newCenter;
}
if (Array == nil) {
  Array = [[NSMutableArray alloc] init];
}
UIImage *bulletImage = [UIImage imageNamed: @"image.png"];
charShot = [[UIImageView alloc] initWithImage: bulletImage];
if (shooting == YES) {
  for(int i=0; i<1; i++) {
    int x = character.center.x + 25;
    int y = character.center.y;
    [self.view addSubview:charShot];
    [Array addObject:charShot];
  }
}
```

That's how you code it. Now that you look at it, doesn't it make you happy that you are using GameSalad? That didn't even include the collisions, muzzle flashes positions, and autodestruction! I'm not even going to begin to explain how to program that... Ok, now let's get back to work.

Time for action – creating bullet collisions

Ok, now that we have all the images created, and the bullets have been brought to life with behaviors, we have to program in the bullet collisions.

1. Let's double-click our **Enemy** actor, and create a new rule. Rename it to Destroy and change the settings to **Actor receives event | overlaps or collides | with actor of type | Bullet**.

2. We want to add some health for these baddies. Under the attributes box of the **Enemy** actor, click the + button to create a new attribute, rename the attribute to Health, and change the value to 4, as shown in the following screenshot:

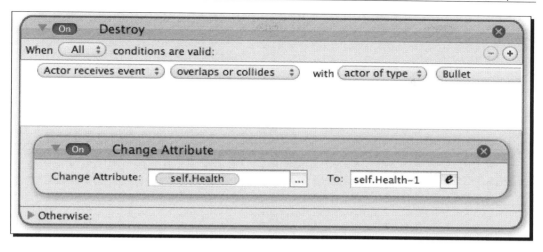

3. Now, drag in a **Change Attribute** behavior, and change the settings to **Change Attribute: | self.Health | To: | self.Health-1**.

4. What this will do is remove 1 health each time a bullet hits it. Easy enough, eh? Now, add in another rule, rename it to `Die` and change it to **Attribute | self.Health | = | 0**.

5. Then, drag in a **Destroy** behavior.

What just happened?

In this section, we created the bullet collisions. When the bullet hits the enemy player, it will reduce the enemy's health. Then when the enemy's health reaches 0, it is destroyed.

Adding some spice to our game

In the last section, we made our player shoot, gave our enemies health, and programmed the destruction of the enemy once their health reaches 0. All is fine and dandy but it doesn't look realistic, when do you ever see something get shot and it just disappears? Unless you are shooting a watermelon with a .50cal, then there really is nothing left. But we aren't shooting watermelons with .50cals! There would be burning twisted wreckage when a mech gets destroyed. So that's what we are going to do, add burning twisted wreckage when our enemy gets blown up.

Time for action – creating burning twisted wreckage

Now, create a wreckage image that will be displayed when the enemy is destroyed, as shown in the following screenshot. I created a twisted and charred wreckage. I took the image of the bad mech, darkened it, and then erased bits and pieces to make it look like it blew apart.

1. Let's import the destroyed wreckage image into GameSalad, and create a new actor and name it Wreckage. We aren't going to import it into the level, we are going to spawn it when the enemy is destroyed, so let's open up our enemy.

2. Drag in a **Spawn Actor** behavior and change the **Actor** to **Wreckage**, as shown in the following screenshot.

3. Test your game to make sure the enemy is destroyed correctly, and the wreckage spawns appropriately (you may have to fiddle around with the rotation and position settings). If everything worked, great! But it's not quite pretty now, is it? First thing you may notice is when the bullet hits the enemy, nothing happens to the bullet!

4. So we have to destroy it, let's edit our **Bullet** actor, create a new rule and rename it Destroy. Change the settings to **Actor receives event | overlaps or collides | with actor of type | Enemy**

5. Now, simply add in a **Destroy** behavior, and that's it. Now, when the bullet hits the enemy it will be destroyed as it should.

6. Let's edit our **Wreckage** actor. Drag in a **Particle** behavior and let's change the settings to the following to make a cool-looking, smouldering, and twisted burning wreckage:

- **Spawn Rate** Tab
  - **Number of Particles**: 100
  - **Particle Startup Time**: 2
  - **Particle Lifetime**: 5

- **Velocity/Position** Tab
  - **Emitter Offset**: 0/0
  - **Direction**: 130 (Relative to scene not actor)
  - **Speed**: 20

- **Size** Tab
  - **Size**: 10 | **Size Changes To** | **Size Transition** Box
    - **Target Size**: 30
    - **Duration**: 3

- **Color** Tab
  - **Color**: Tangerine (Or a tint of orange or yellow that you prefer)
  - **Color Changes to**
  - **Blending**: Additive
  - **Color Transition** Box | **Target Color**: Black
  - **Duration**: 5

- **Rotation** Tab
  - **Initial Rotation**: 0
  - **Angular Velocity**: 0

- **Image** Tab
  - **Set Image to**: (Then, select our smoke image, or another one you like)

Then, as seen in the next screenshot, the final result looks pretty cool!

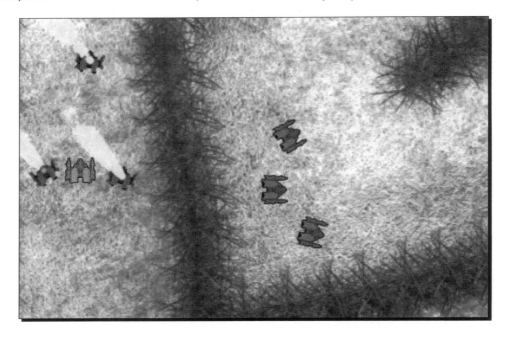

Creating Our AI

The game would be no fun if we could just go running around killing some baddies without them putting up a fight, right? Yeah no challenge whatsoever, so we are going to add in some AI (artificial intelligence); simple-minded AI, but they can be challenging when they are raining a barrage of bullets at you, right? Okay! Hmmm where to start...

Time for action – AI Detection (lines of sight)

This is going to be pretty complex and it's not going to be 100 percent perfect, but it's a great way for a new user starting out.

1. In the **Scene Editor**, click the **Attributes** tab in the **Inspector**, and create three new attributes:

- ❏ **PlayerX | Integer**
- ❏ **PlayerY | Integer**
- ❏ **PlayerR | Integer**

2. Next, go into the **Enemy** actor and delete the **Spawn Actor** behavior that we created earlier.

3. What we have to do now is create a new attribute within our **Enemy** actor, and name it `Noticed`. Create a new rule and rename it `Noticed`. Let's change the settings to **Actor receives event | overlaps or collides | with actor of type | Detector**

4. Then let's drag in a **Change Attribute** behavior and change it to **Attribute | self. Noticed | is | true**.

5. Take a look at the following screenshot to see if you filled out everything properly.

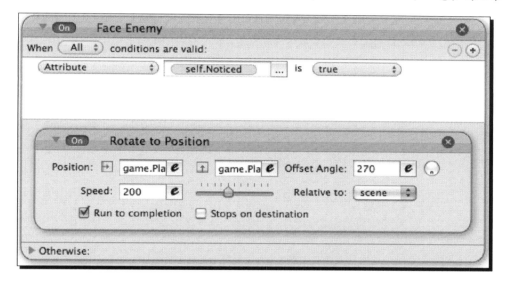

6. Open the **Otherwise** roll-out, copy that **Change Attribute** behavior and change it from **true** to **false**.

7. Double-click our **Detector** actor, and we are going to drag in two **Constrain Attribute** behaviors here, one will be **Constrain Attribute: | self.Position.X | To: | game.PlayerX and** the second will be **Constrain Attribute: | self.Position.Y | To: | game.PlayerY**

8. And now, we are going to add in a **Rotate to Angle** behavior and change it to:

   - **Angle:** `game.PlayerR`
   - **Speed:** `10000`

9. Uncheck the **Stops on Destination** box, so that it will rotate constantly. Basically, what that will do is make the detector follow the player around the map and rotate in the direction he is facing, simple right?

10. Go back to the **Scene Editor** and drag in our **Detector** actor on top of our player.

11. We now have to add in a couple behaviors to change the player position attributes, which we created. Double-click the **Player** actor, let's drag in a **Timer** behavior, change it to **Every**: 0.001 **seconds**

12. Then, add in three **Change Attribute** behaviors, and we are going to change them to:

    First change attribute: **Change Attribute: | game.PlayerX | To: | self.Position.X**

    Second change attribute: **Change Attribute: | game.PlayerY | To: | self.Position.Y**

    Third change attribute: **Change Attribute: | game.PlayerR | To: | self.Rotation**

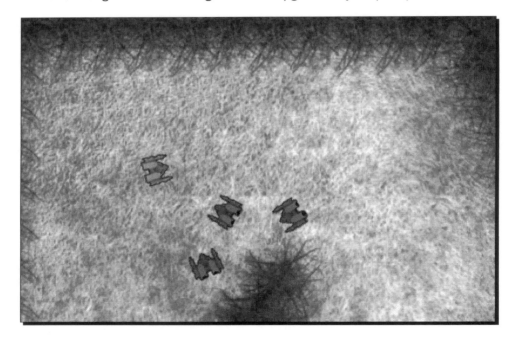

Ah, locked and loaded! Okay, that's just a little scary. Now, let the shooting begin! Austin Powers quote there, but it works well.

13. Let's go into our **Enemy** actor, and in our **Face Enemy** rule, add a **Timer** behavior and change it to **Every** 0.5 **seconds**. Next, drag in a **Spawn Actor** behavior, select the **Bullet** actor, and then for the Y Position change it to 50, and for the X Position change it to -8.

14. Make three copies of this behavior, change the X Position in the second one to 8, then in the third and fourth behavior, change the actor from **Bullet** to **Muzzle Flash** (which will spawn the Muzzle Flash instead of a Bullet), and the **Direction** to self. Rotation. Take a look at the following screenshot to see what I mean.

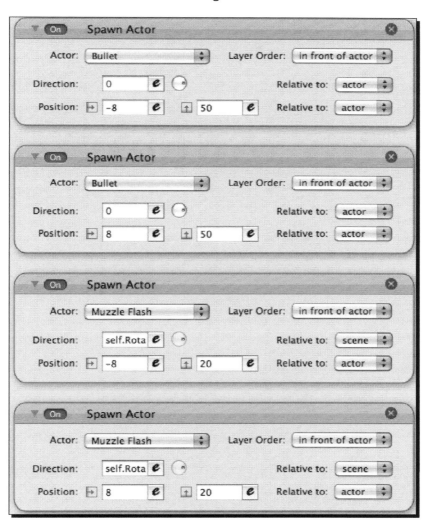

15. Save your work and test it to see if everything works well; if not, take a look at the previous screenshot to see if all your settings were correct.

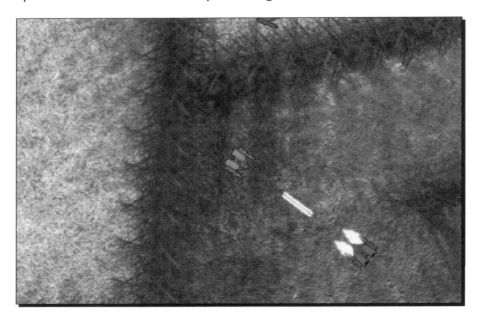

The previous screenshot should be your final outcome, the bad guys are pelting you with bullets, and it looks pretty good too!

What just happened?

In this section, we created enemies that can now detect the player. Once they come close, they will rotate to your position, and then they will start to shoot.

Adding spice to our player and UI

Earlier we gave our enemies health, but now we have to give our player some health. This will be done approximately the same way as we did for our enemies, but in addition to that we are going to add some user interface elements.

Time for action – creating player health, and a HUD

Now, we need to create health for our player:

1. Let's drag in our **HUD** (heads up display) actor into the scene. Double-click it, open up the **Graphics** rollout and change the **Blending Mode** to Additive.

2. Go back to our scene, and in the **Inspector**, click the **Scene** button. Then, go to the **Layers** tab and click the **+** button to create a new layer, name this one HUDs. Rearrange it so it is at top of the **Background** layer, then check off **Scrollable**, because we want this layer to follow the camera.

3. Let's expand the **Background** layer and find the **HUD** actor and drag it into our new **HUD** layer. Now, we have to give our player some health. Click the **Attributes** tab in the **Inspector**. Let's create a new attribute by clicking the **+** button, make it an **Integer**, rename it to Health, and change the value to 143.

4. Next, we have to create a new actor, name it Health Bar, and then double-click it so we can edit it. In the **Attributes** box, change the **Color** to Spring, which is a nice green, change the **Width** to 15 and **Height** to 143 and in the **Graphics** roll-out change the **Blending Mode** to Additive. Now, let's drag in a **Constrain Attribute** and change the settings to **Constrain Attribute: | self.Size.Height | To: | game.Health**.

5. Then, add a new rule, call it Reset Level, and let's change it to the following:

   Attribute | game.Health... | Less or equal to (the underlined <) **| 0**

6. Next, drag in a simple **Reset Scene** behavior. Now for one final touch we have to go into our **Bullet** actor, and clone our **Destroy** rule, and in the rule change **Enemy** to Player.

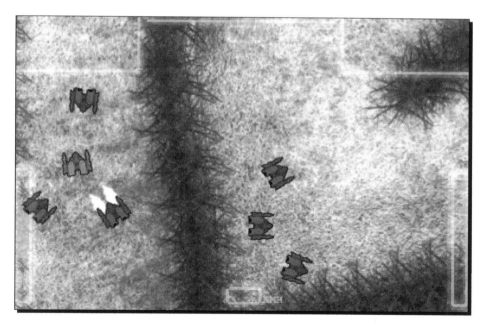

Look at them just chipping away at our health! This is fun, isn't it?

What just happened?

We created some health for our player, and created a HUD that reflected our player's health. When the player's health reaches 0, it will restart the level.

Rockets, smoke, and explosions, oh my!

What mech game would be complete without ROCKETS?! None of them! GameSalad allows us to do some pretty complex things, such as targeting, but I'm going to keep it easy. If you exited the **Scene Editor**, not to worry, but we need to go back into it.

Time for action – creating the rockets

1. Import the rocket image that is in the resources section of this book (shown in the following screenshot), or you can create your own:

2. Create a new actor from the image simply by dragging the image into the **Inspector**, or by clicking the + button to create a new actor and drag the image into it (but I prefer the first option and I'm sure you do too), and name it Rocket.

3. Double-click the new actor so we can edit it, there are going to be a few behaviors for the rocket.

4. First off, we are going to create a two-stage kind of rocket, so drag in an **Accelerate** behavior, and change it to the following:

    ❑   **Direction**: 90

    ❑   **Acceleration**: 100

The given settings can be seen in the following screenshot:

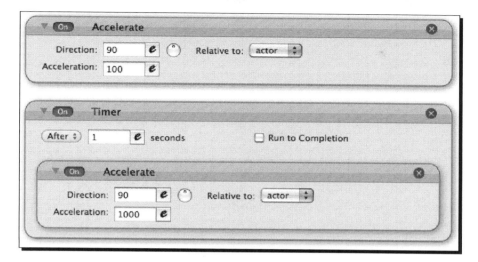

 Also make sure the **Relative To:** drop-down box has **Actor** selected; if you have **Scene** selected it will accelerate to the top of the screen no matter what, instead of accelerating forward in the direction the actor is facing.

5. Now, let's add in a **Timer** behavior, let's change the settings to **After:** 1 **seconds**. Then, duplicate the **Accelerate** behavior we created earlier and place it within the **Timer** behavior, and simply change the **Acceleration** from 100 to 1000.

What just happened?

Now, if you place one of these rockets in the scene and play the level you will see it launches and then it takes off, like a real rocket! COOL!

Time for action – creating particle effects

Now, we are going to add some cool particle effects. We are again going to create a two-stage rocket here. We are going to create two particle behaviors, one for the rocket flames, and the other for the rocket smoke.

1. Let's start with the flames. Change the settings to the following:

- ◆ **Spawn Rate** Tab
    - ❑ **Number of Particles**: 200
    - ❑ **Particle Startup Time**: 0
    - ❑ **Particle Lifetime**: 0.5 **seconds**
- ◆ **Velocity/Position** Tab
    - ❑ **Speed**: 0
- ◆ **Size** Tab
    - ❑ **Size**: 5
    - ❑ **Size Changes to**
    - ❑ **Target Size**: 1
    - ❑ **Duration**: 0.3 **seconds**
- ◆ **Color** Tab:
    - ❑ **Color**: Lemon
    - ❑ **Blending**: Additive
- ◆ **Image** Tab:
    - ❑ **Set Image to**: Smoke

2. Now, we are going to create another **Particle** behavior, and we are going to use the following settings:

- ◆ **Spawn Rate** Tab
    - ❑ **Number of Particles**: 500
    - ❑ **Particle Startup Time**: 2
    - ❑ **Particle Lifetime**: 1 **seconds**

- ◆ **Velocity/Position** Tab
  - ❑ **Speed**: 0
- ◆ **Size** Tab
  - ❑ **Size**: 5
  - ❑ **Size Changes to**
  - ❑ **Target Size**: 100
  - ❑ **Duration**: 1 seconds
- ◆ **Color** Tab:
  - ❑ **Color**: Iron
  - ❑ **Blending**: Normal
- ◆ **Image** Tab:
  - ❑ **Set Image to**: Smoke

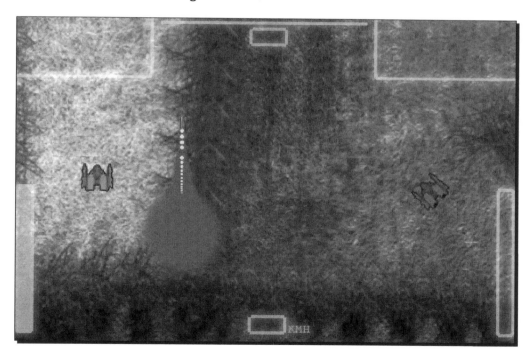

3. See how the rocket looks in the previous image. Pretty good huh? You can fiddle around with the particle settings to get it looking just the way you like. Now, we are going to edit our **Player** actor.

4. Create a new rule and change the settings to **Actor receives event key** (select a key that you would like to use. This is temporary, as we will be getting to the iPhone controls soon enough) **is pressed**. Name the rule `Shooting Rockets`, drag in a **Spawn Actor** behavior, change the settings to:

- **Actor**: `Rocket`
- **Direction**: `self.Rotation`
- **Position X**: `-8`
- **Position Y**: `20`

5. Next we are going to duplicate the **Spawn Actor** behavior and simply change the actor to **Muzzle Flash** instead of **Rocket**.

Ahh! Rockets flying all over the place in the previous screenshot, now we have to add in the destruction!!! (*evil laugh*)

What just happened?

In this section, we created some very cool-looking particle effects for the rockets! We created flame particles and then created big plumes of smoke that gradually get bigger in size, like a real rocket!

Time for action – particle explosions!

Now that we have the rockets flying all around, we are going to create the destruction, mainly explosions! (*another evil laugh*!!)

1. Ok, enough of that. Now, in our **Enemy** actor, we need to add in our rocket/enemy collisions, so double-click our **Enemy** actor. Let's create a new rule and name it `Rocket Collision`; change it to **Actor Receives event | overlaps or collides | with actor of type | Rocket**.

2. Now, we are going to drag in a **Change Attribute** and change it to **Change Attribute: | self.Health | To: | self.Health** `-4`

This will kill our enemy in one hit, which seems about right for a rocket or an RPG.

3. We have to create a new actor that will act as our explosion. In our **Inspector** click the **+** button, and name our new actor `Explosion`. Double-click our actor and add in a **Particle** behavior, changing the settings to the following:

- ◆ **Spawn Rate** Tab
  - ❑ **Number of Particles:** 50
  - ❑ **Particle Startup Time:** 0
  - ❑ **Particle Lifetime:** 0.5 **seconds**

- ◆ **Velocity/Position** Tab
  - ❑ **Speed:** 0

- ◆ **Size** Tab
  - ❑ **Size:** 10
  - ❑ **Size Changes To:**
  - ❑ **Target Size:** 200
  - ❑ **Duration:** 0.5 **seconds**

- **Color** Tab:
    - ❑ **Color**: Iron
    - ❑ **Color Changes to:**
    - ❑ **Target Color:** Licorice
    - ❑ **Blending:** Normal

- **Image** Tab:
    - ❑ **Set Image to:** Smoke

4. Now, we are going to drag in another **Particle** behavior for the flames, and we are going to use the following settings:

- **Spawn Rate** Tab
    - ❑ **Number of Particles**: 50
    - ❑ **Particle Startup Time**: 0
    - ❑ **Particle Lifetime**: 2.5 **seconds**

- **Velocity/Position** Tab
    - ❑ **Speed**: 0

- **Size** Tab
    - ❑ **Size**: 5
    - ❑ **Size Changes to**
    - ❑ **Target Size**: 150
    - ❑ **Duration**: 2.5 **seconds**

- **Color** Tab:
    - ❑ **Color**: Lemon
    - ❑ **Color changes to**
    - ❑ **Target Color**: Cayenne
    - ❑ **Blending**: Additive

- **Image** Tab:
    - ❑ **Set Image to**: Smoke

5. Now, let's go back into our **Rocket** actor, so we can add a new rule, change it to **Actor receives event | overlaps or collides | with actor of type | Enemy**

6. Let's drag in a **Spawn Actor** and change the **Actor** to **Explosion**, and then drag in a **Destroy** behavior under the **Spawn Actor** behavior, just to ensure the spawns explode before we destroy our rocket. See the effect in the following screenshot. I think it looks good, but again, you can play around with it to make it look as cool as you want.

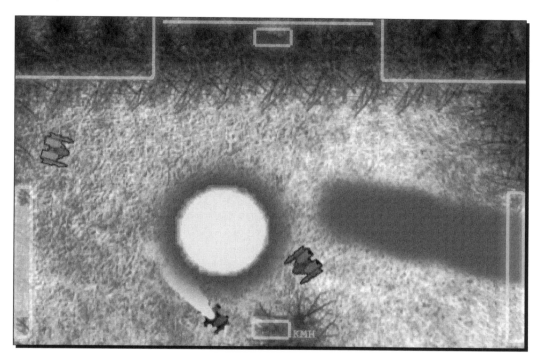

What just happened?

In this section, we looked at creating particle explosions when a rocket hits an enemy. We created two particle behaviors, one for the smoke and one for the flames/explosion.

Adding more interface elements

Now, we are going to look at adding some more UI spice! These won't affect the game whatsoever, but they look really cool and what you learn will come in handy in many other types of games, such as racing, air-combat, and even RPG's!

Time for action – creating speedometer and a compass

We are going to create a speedometer to show how fast you are going, and then we are going to create a compass to show what direction you are facing. Let's dive right into it.

1. Create a new actor and name it Speedometer. Double-click it and we are going to edit it a bit. Change the **Width** and **Height** to 32, and in the **Attributes** box, click the **+** button to add a new attribute. Click the **Integer** selector and click **OK**, and name it Speed.

2. Let's drag in a **Display Text** and change the **text** field to self.Speed, the **size** to 15 and the **color** to Lime. Then create a new rule, name it Speed Up, and change it to **Actor receives event | key | up | is down**.

3. Next, drag in a **Timer** behavior, change it to **For** 2 **seconds**, and then drag in another **Timer** behavior and change it to **Every** 0.001 **seconds**. Then drag in a **Change Attribute** behavior and change the behavior to **Change Attribute: | self.Speed | To: | self.Speed+1**.

4. Next, expand the **Otherwise** roll-out and duplicate the **Change Attribute** behavior, changing to **Change Attribute: | self.Speed | To: | 0**.

5. As with all the other steps, take a look at the next screenshot to see if you filled out everything correctly.

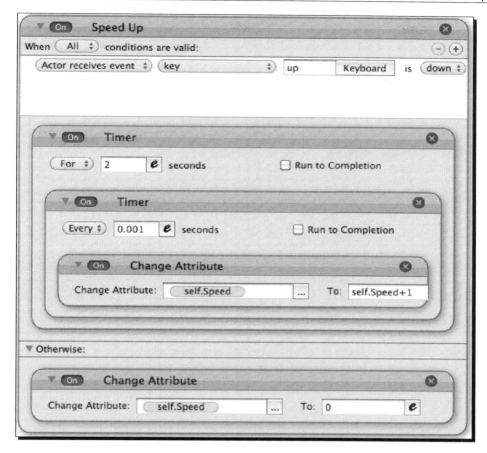

6. Now, drag our **Speedometer** into the relevant box of our HUD. Make sure that it is in the **HUD** layer, so it follows the camera. Then duplicate the **Speedometer** actor and rename it Compass.

7. Double-click it so we can edit it. Delete the **Speed Up** rule and change the **Display Text** behavior's **Text** field to `game.PlayerR`. Go back to the **Scene Editor** and drag it into the **Compass** part of our HUD.

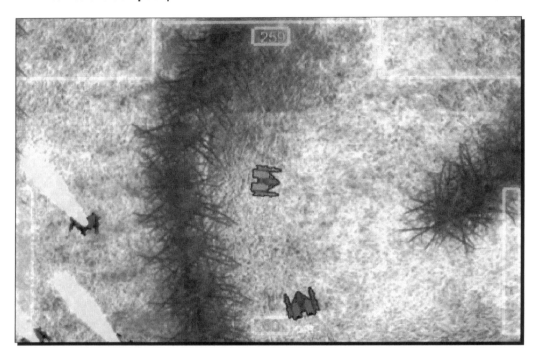

The previous screenshot shows the final product, the burning twisted wreckage and the enemies detecting us when we get close. We also have a compass and a speedometer!

What just happened?

We added some spice to our user interface by creating a simple speedometer and a compass. The compass can be used for objective-type missions when you want the player to get to a certain area in the map.

That's it for this chapter my friend! I hope you learned a lot from it. In the next chapter, we are going to finish up the game mechanics, and add in the second level with the turrets and more! We are almost done! Prepare yourself for another fun chapter, I'll see you there!

Pop quiz

1. How would you create an image that looks like it's glowing?

    a. In your imaging software, create an image with a Gaussian blur. Then, in GS add an Additive Blending Mode

    b. In your imaging software, create a "Pixelated" filter. Then, in GS, add an Opaque Blending Mode

    c. In your imaging software, create a "Bloom" filter. Then, in GS, add a behavior that will set the Bloom Effect to On

    d. None of the above

2. True or False: GameSalad can do complex things such as targeting

    a. True

    b. False

3. How would you create bullets?

    a. Within GameSalad, you must create an NSMutableArray then code them within a timer

    b. Create a Spawn Actor Behavior within a timer to constantly spawn, or outside of one just to spawn once

    c. Create a shoot Behavior within the bullet's behaviors

    d. None of the above

Summary

In this chapter, we learned some very important things that can be used in any game, such as shooting bullets and rockets, particle effects, enemy detection, speedometer, and compasses. As mentioned before, GameSalad makes all these things super easy, things that when coded in Xcode or any other SDK can take many, and I mean MANY lines of code. In the next chapter, we are going to finish off the main mechanics of the game. We are going to create one more level and we are even going to look at creating some turrets!

10
Metal Mech Part 3

We are getting closer and closer to finishing this awesome project, aren't we? This part is going to complete the gameplay, finish all the core mechanics of the game and get it all ready and pretty-looking for release on the App Store.

So, let's take a look at what we are going to cover in this chapter:

- ◆ Level collisions
- ◆ Sound effects
- ◆ Turrets
- ◆ Weapon overheating
- ◆ Scoring
- ◆ Mission briefing (in the UI)
- ◆ iPhone controls!

We are so close to finishing the main mechanics for this game and it is getting so exciting! By the end of this chapter, it will be a fully functional game for your computer, Let's get to it!

Creating Level 1 collisions

Until now, because we haven't programmed in the level collisions, we have just been able to walk right through the tree line. Obviously we don't want this to happen, not only would it be unfair (because the player would walk through the tree line, and the enemies could shoot right through) but it's also physically impossible to walk through a tree.

Time for action – creating level bounds

Now, we are going to create the level bounds. These will be invisible actors that will be in areas we don't want our player to walk, similar to the tree lines or buildings, and so on.

1. What we have to do is, go into our **Scene Editor**, and in the **Inspector** we create a new actor and name it Level Bounds or something to that effect, something easy to remember.

2. Now, double-click it so we can edit our actor. Then, in the **Attributes** box, open up the **Physics** roll-out, uncheck the **Movable** box, and change the **Restitution** (bounciness) to 0. We want to do this because we don't want it to move around once the player collides with it. The following screenshot shows the settings made in the **Attributes** box:

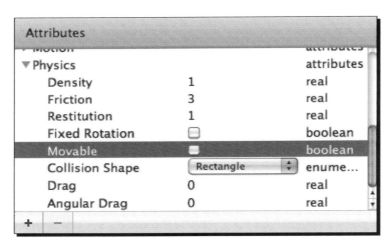

3. Drag in a **Change Attribute** behavior, and change it to **Change Attribute: | self.Color. Alpha | To: | 0**.

   The settings are shown in the following screenshot:

4. Now, all we have to do is go back to the **Scene Editor** and drag this actor all around the bounds and obstacles of our levels, in all the places that we don't want our player to walk through. You will need to stretch and rotate them all around, and make sure you don't have any jagged edges between two actors because this will cause awkward collisions and jumping for our character.

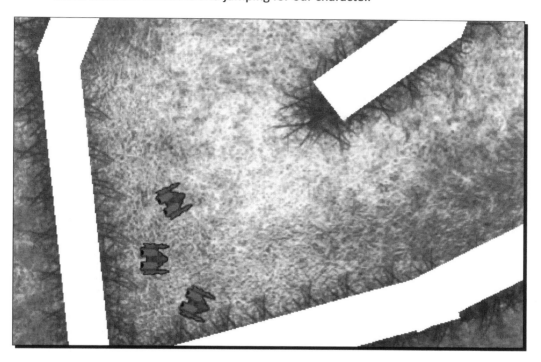

5. Look at the lower-right corner of the previous screenshot. Make sure that you round it out like the collider at the upper-left of the image. Now, let's go into our **Player** actor, drag in a **Collide** behavior, and change it to **Bounce | when colliding with: | actor of type: | Level Bounds**.

6. This is going to stop our player when it collides into the actor; it's so simple, isn't it? I would take one simple behavior over 10 lines of code for a simple collision (hint Xcode). Now, we have to change the bounciness of our player; so, in the **Attributes** box change the **Restitution** to 0.

7. Test the game and you will see our player will stop when we hit the bounds. Now, we have to do the same for our bullets, and the rockets.

8. Let's start with the bullets first, so go into our **Bullet** actor. We need to create a new rule and name it to `Collide with Bounds`, change the rule settings to **Actor receives event | overlaps or collides | with actor of type | Level Bounds**

9. Simply drag in a **Destroy** behavior and that's it! Now, go into our **Rocket** and duplicate our **Destroy** behavior that we had in there before, but change the **Rule** from **Enemy**, to **Level Bounds**.

It's that easy! Now, let's test it out to make sure that everything works.

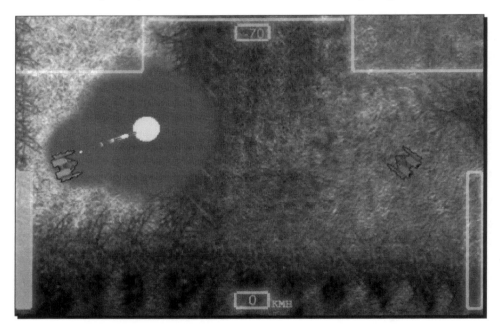

10. As you can see, the rocket was destroyed as soon as it hit our level bound. So perfect! Everything worked well. Now for one more thing that we have to do for this level and that is, add in a way to go to the next level. So, let's create a new actor, and name it **Next Level**. Now, we have to edit this new actor.

11. Firstly, we have to drag in a **Change Attribute** behavior in which we will be changing the **alpha** to 0. If you forget, you have to change the settings to **Change Attribute: | self.Color.Alpha | To: | 0**.

12. Create a new rule and change it to **Actor receives event | overlaps or collides | with actor of type | Player**.

13. Finally, drag in a **Change Scene** behavior into that rule, and now we have to drag it into our scene, right at the end of our level, which is where the compound is (the big gray box).

What just happened?

In this section, we created the level bounds to prevent our player from walking in areas such as tree lines, buildings, or rocks.

Test your level every time you do something new to make sure that it works well. Also remember to save your work frequently (and it could save your life... not really, but it will save you big headaches) and even create backups regularly just in case you get a crash. I've had it happen before and I lost months of work on one small crash *HEADACHE!*. On to the sound effects! Just as a recap, in this section, we added level bounds in which our player, enemies, bullets, and rockets will collide with. This will prevent cheating from the player, and the enemies shooting you through the tree line.

Creating sound effects!

If you haven't already, download the sound effects for this section, or if you would like, you can download your own.

1. We are going to go into our **Player** actor. In the **Keyboard Movement** group, find our **Shooting Bullets** rule. Under the **Timer** behavior, drag in a **Play Sound** behavior and select our **Gun** sound effect. This can be seen in the following screenshot:

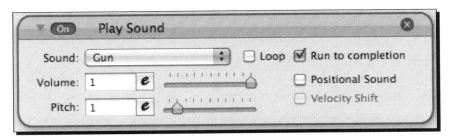

2. Also, do the same for our rockets firing. Drag in a **Play Sound** behavior in our **Shooting Rockets** group, and change it to **Rocket**. Don't forget that, when you import your sound effects into GameSalad, you have the option to import it as a sound effect or a music file, just keep it in mind.

3. Finally, for our player, in our **Hit** roll-out, drag in a **Play Sound** behavior with our **Ricochet** sound effect.

4. Next, we have to focus on our **Enemy** actor, so we add in our **Ricochet.wav** sound effect into its **Bullet Collision** group. We are going to select **Positional Sound**, which is pretty self-explanatory, but essentially it's 3D sound; the closer the sound effect is to the camera the louder it will be, the further away it is, the quieter it will be. Think of a speaker playing music, as you walk away from it, it sounds quieter, but the closer you are to it, the louder it is. This is positional sound; the volume is determined by the position of the actor playing the sound effect.

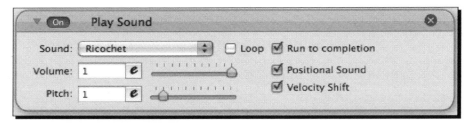

5. We also have to add in our **Gun sound effect** into our **Face Enemy** group, under the **Timer**. Do the same with this behavior as with the last one. Click off the **Positional Sound**, and if you like, also the **Velocity Shift** box. Just play around with the settings to see what sounds better to you.

6. Finally, for our **Enemy** actor, we have to add in our **Explosion.wav** sound effect into the **Rocket Collision** behavior.

7. Now, let's go do our **Rocket** behavior in our first **Destroy** rule (the one where we detect a collision with the **Level Bounds**). Drag in our **Explosion** sound effect, and if you like, check off the **Positional Sound** and **Velocity Shift**, if it sounds good to you.

8. Now, just one more thing for this level, double-click our background image **Level 1** and drag in our **BattleSounds** music file, and check off the **Loop** box. Now, when you test our level, it is filled with wonderful gritty battle sounds! If only you could hear it through the book, hmm... If only this page had one of those sound boxes as in the children's books! Oh well, moving on...

 To add some more zest to this game, why not use different sound effects for the collisions? Things such as wood splintering when a bullet hits the trees, or a metal clank when a bullet hits a metal wall.

Creating turrets in a new level

Now, we are going to create a new level, and in this one we are going to have turrets! These, similar to the enemy mechs, will detect you and turn and start shooting at you when you get close.

1. Create a new level (in the project's home screen click the **+** button) and rename it `Level 2`. Now, we have to populate it with all our actors as shown in the following screenshot (this isn't the whole level by the way):

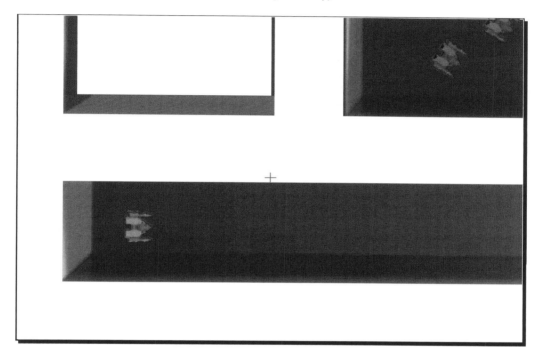

2. Now, we are going to work on blowing the breath of life into our turrets. If you notice, we put the level colliders on top of our turrets. So, in the **Inspector** with the **Scene** button selected, click the **Layers** tab.

3. Scroll through the list and click on each **Turret** actor you see, which will select that actor within the scene. Then, find the selected one in the scene, right-click it, and then click **Send to Front**. Alternately you can press *Shift +Command + "+"*, which is easier if you cannot right-click because something is in the way, or the actor is too small.

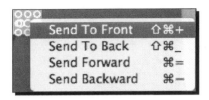

Now that all of them are shown, it will make it easier to select and move them around if needed.

4. Let's open up the **Turret** that is in the **Inspector**, so we can edit it. Create a new rule, name it `Face Player`, and change the settings to **Actor receives event | overlaps or collides | with actor of type | Detector.**

5. Now, drag in a **Rotate to Position** behavior and change the settings to the following:

   - **Position X**: `game.PlayerX`
   - **Position Y**: `game.PlayerY`
   - **Offset Angle**: `270`
   - **Speed**: `100` (or whatever you think would be an appropriate speed)
   - **Relative to**: `scene`
   - **Stops on Destination**: `off`

6. Let's save our work and test it out, just to make sure it works.

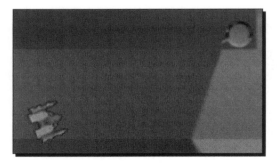

If it works, great! But if it doesn't, go back to the code to make sure that everything was typed in correctly, because when you're going quickly, it's so easy to miss one thing, and even easier to pass over it many times trying to fix it! Just take your time.

Time for action – making the turrets fire!

In this section, we are going to make our cute little turrets fire at us. Ok, maybe they aren't as cute as the turrets in Portal 2. Moving on, in this section, we are going to—similar to the mechs—create a line of sight for the turrets, and then we are going to make them shoot, and program how to destroy them.

1. Drag in a **Timer** behavior. Change it to **Every** 0.25 **seconds** (I know that's a very quick rate of fire, but hey, it will be a little bit of a challenge). We are going to start off by playing a sound effect. Drag in a **Play Sound** behavior and change it to **Gun**, then make sure **Run to completion**, **Positional Sound**, and **Velocity Shift** are all on. These are pretty much all the same behaviors as our **Enemy** actor.

2. Next, we are going to drag in a **Spawn Actor** behavior, change the actor to **Bullet**, and change the Y Position to 50. Then click *Option* and left-click that behavior to duplicate it, and change the **Actor** to Muzzle Flash, the **Direction** to self. Rotation, and the Y Position to 20.

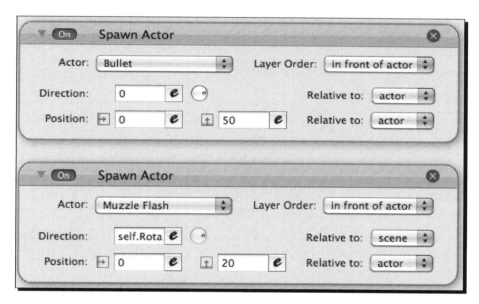

Now, our turret will be shooting at us! But we need to be able to defend ourselves by shooting back. So, let's add in the collisions.

3. For killing the turrets, create a new rule and change it to this **Actor receives event | overlaps or collides | with actor of type | Bullet**.

4. Then, drag in a **Spawn Actor** behavior, and change it to `Explosion`. Also, drag in a **Play Sound** behavior and change it to `Explosion`, and check on **Positional Sound**.

5. Finally, drag in a **Destroy** behavior. Now, all we have to do is click *Option* and left-click that **Bullet Collision** rule to duplicate it, and simply rename it to `Rocket Collision` and change the rule to **Actor receives event | overlaps or collides | with actor of type | Rocket**.

What just happened?

In this section, we looked at creating turrets that have a line of sight, will look at you when you pass by, then start shooting at you.

Have a go hero

For this part, why not create a destroyed turret image similar to the one drawn for the mechs, so when you hit them, instead of them just disappearing, they spawn a new destroyed image.

As with every time we finish a section, save your work and test the level just to make sure it works. If so, let's move on!

Weapon overheating, and more UI fun!

Now, let's add in and finish the UI:

1. In our second level, let's create a new layer in the **Inspector**, name it `HUD`, and uncheck the **Scrollable** box.

2. Next, drag in our **HUD** actor, along with our **Health Bar**. Then we have to create another bar, but we are just going to duplicate our **Health Bar**. Again to do this, *Option* + left-click and left-click the **Health Bar**, rename it to `Heat Bar`.

3. Click on the **Attributes** tab in the **Inspector**, click the "+" button to create one, select **Integer** and then click **OK**. Rename it to Heat, and change the **Integer** to 0, if it's not already.

4. Next, we have to edit the **Heat Bar** actor, change the **Constrain Attribute** behavior to **Constrain Attribute: | self.Size.Height | To: | game.Heat**.

5. Let's create a new rule, rename it Change Color, then change the settings to **Attribute game.Heat > 100**.

6. Drag in two **Change Attribute** behaviors, change the first one to **Change Attribute: | self.Color.Green | To: | 0**, and the second one to **Change Attribute: | self.Color.Red | To: | 1**.

7. Simply duplicate the **Change Color** rule and switch it around so that it's less than or equal to 100, and change the **Green** to 1 and the **Red** to 0.

8. Now, we have to go back to our **Player** actor, open up the **Keyboard Movement** group, and then open up the **Shooting Bullets** rule. Click the little + button in the rule to create another condition of the rule, and change the new rule to **Attribute game.Heat < 143**.

   Creating a new condition within a rule can add a lot of functionality. The settings are shown in the following screenshot:

9. Then, drag in a **Change Attribute** behavior and change the settings to **Change Attribute: | game.Heat | To: | game.Heat + 5**.

10. Now, do the same for the **Shooting Rockets**, but instead of adding 5 heats per shot, let's do 35.75. Then, drag in a **Timer** behavior, rename it to Cool Down and change it to **Every** 0.5 **seconds**, drag in a **Change Attribute** behavior and change that to **Change Attribute: | game.Heat | To: | game.Heat − 10**.

11. Save it and let's give it a try. Check to see that everything works ok, as in the following screenshot; if so, let's keep going.

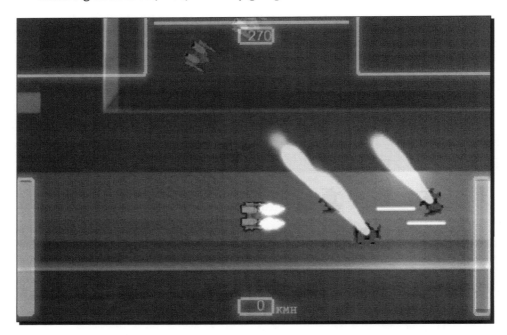

Perfect! Now, we are going to continue the rest of the UI, mainly the scoring and the mission/objective monitor.

Now, let's create a new attribute for our mission log:

1. In the **Inspector**, with the **Game** button selected, click the **Attributes** tab and click the **+** button to create a new attribute. Select **Text**, then click **OK**, then rename it to Mission.

2. Go back to the **Actors** tab, and click the **+** button to create a new actor and rename it Mission, then double-click it so we can edit it. Change the **Width** to **130** and **Heigth** to **64**.

3. Simply drag in a **Display Text** attribute, change the **Text** field to **game.Mission**. Now, change the **Font** to **Arial** and the **Size** to 10, and the **Color** to **Licorice**, or if you want you can change it to any color you like, something that would be visible on all backgrounds; this is your creation!

4. Finally, change the **Alpha** to 0, and the **Blending Mode** to Additive. Drag it into our scene in the upper-right corner of our **HUD**, and save your project.

5. If you test it now, you will see absolutely nothing, mainly because, we haven't filled in any text for our mission. So, let's go to our **Level 1 – Objectives** scene. Find the **Level1Objective** actor in the scene, this is the background image for this scene. Double-click it and drag in a **Change Attribute** behavior. Now, let's change the settings to **Change Attribute: | game.Mission | To: |** (Insert any mission goals).

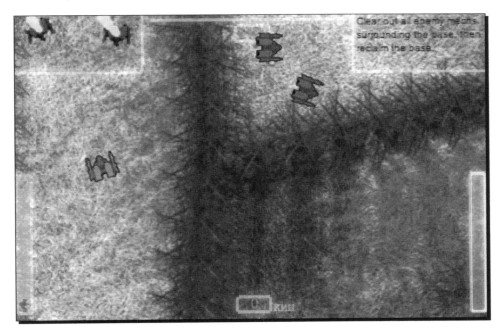

6. The way we have set up the mission log makes it very simple to change when a new mission comes along. There's no need to create a new actor every time, all you have to do is add in a **Change Attribute** behavior like we did, and just change the text, it's that easy.

Now, let's focus on the scoring, which will be as easy as the mission log:

1. Back in the **Attributes** section, let's create a new one, select **Integer**, and change the name to `Score`.

2. Now, go back to the **Actors** tab, duplicate our **Mission** actor by clicking *Option* + left-clicking it, and then rename it to `Score`.

3. Double-click the **Score** actor and change the **Display Text** box to `game.Score`, and that's all that we need to do with this actor aside from adding it to our scene, so go back to our **Scene Editor** and drag in our **Score** actor into the upper-left corner of our **HUD**.

4. Now, let's go edit our **Enemy** actor and under our **Die** rule, drag in a **Change Attribute** behavior and change it to **Change Attribute: | game.Score | To: | game. Score + 100**.

5. Now, we are going to make it a little more fair by implementing a rule that when we get hit by a bullet we will lose 50 points. Double-click our **Bullet** actor, create a new rule and change it to **Actor receives event | overlaps or collides | with actor of type | Player**.

6. Now, click the little **+** button under the **x** button in the rule, and change that condition to **Attribute | game.Score | > | 0**.

   The settings are shown in the following screenshot:

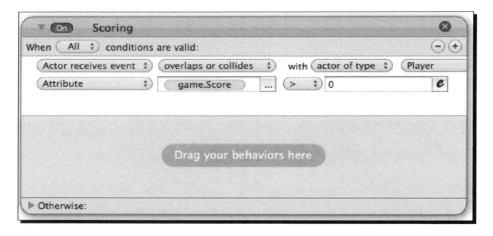

7. Now, similar to the previous screenshot, let's drag in a **Change Attribute** behavior and change it to **Change Attribute: | game.Score | To: | game.Score − 50**.

8. So simple, isn't it! That's all that we need to do for that! Now, the rest is up to you!

The following screenshot shows what we have done in this example:

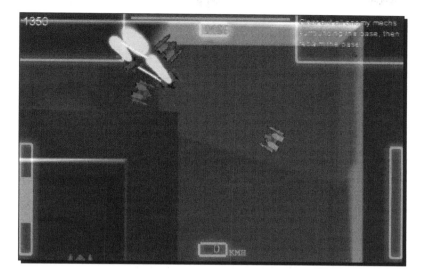

Have a go hero

This whole time you had a nice guideline to follow of what to do, but now that you have a good knowledge of GameSalad, why not take matters into your own hands? Add some more functionality to the game; why not add a health bar that follows our player around, kind of like a bar under our player so our player doesn't have to take his/her eyes off the action to see check the health score? Or why not have the player's name displayed above the player, as shown in the following screenshot:

Continue the story too, make it a compelling story, one that people will want to play, you know some bizarre twist of events where you find out that it's your father who is the head of the evil corporation and now you have to defeat him.

iPhone controls!

Now that we are finished with the main parts of the game, we have to start getting it ready for the iPhone, don't we? The main thing that we have to do is the controls. The worst thing that we could do is deploy the game to the App Store without incorporating any controls. So, let's dive right into the touch controls.

Time for action – touch controls

We are going to start off with some simple touch controls. Basically, we are going to create buttons in the scene. When we touch these buttons they will turn on a Boolean that will be detected in our actor, which will trigger a shooting behavior.

1. Let's go to our first playable level; we have to drag in our two buttons (guns and rockets) into the scene.

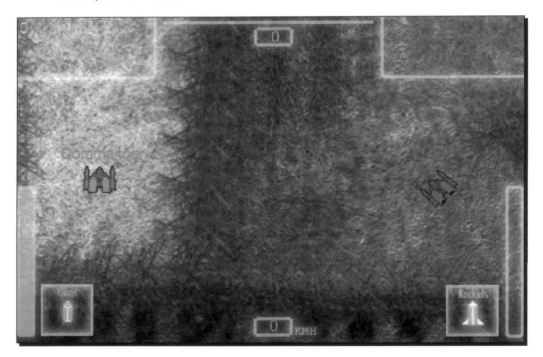

2. Now, we have to create two new attributes, one `Gun-Shooting` and the second `Rocket-Shooting` (both Booleans). Let's go edit our **Gun Button** actor, we have to create a rule and name it `Is Touched?` Change it to **Actor receives event | touch | is | pressed**.

3. Then, drag in a **Change Attribute** behavior and change it to **Change Attribute: | game.Gun-Shooting | To: | true**.

4. Now, expand the **Otherwise** drop-down box in the rule, then duplicate the **Change Attribute** behavior into the **Otherwise** box, and change it to `false`. Do the same for the **Rocket Button**, but of course change it to **game.Rocket-Shooting**.

5. Next, go into the **Player** actor and copy the **Shooting Bullets/Shooting Rockets** rules that are in the **Keyboard Movement**; we are going to create a new group and name it `iPhone Movement` and paste in those shooting rules. Change the **Shooting Bullets** rule to **Attribute: | game.Gun-Shooting | is | true**.

6. Also, change the **Shooting Rockets** rule to **Attribute: | game.Rocket-Shooting | is | true**.

What just happened?

In this section, we created two on-screen buttons, when touched will turn on the Booleans that we created, and then when you release the button it will turn the Booleans off. These Booleans will be used in our Player actor to detect if the user is pressing the button, if so, fire accordingly.

Time for action - iPhone acceleration

For this section, we are going to use the iPhone's accelerometer to move our player back and forth.

1. Within the **iPhone Movement** group, create a new rule and name it **Accelerometer**, changing the settings to **Attribute: | game.Accelerometer.X | > |** 0.

2. Then, we drag in a **Move** behavior and change the settings to:
   - **Direction:** 90
   - **Speed:** 100

Everything else can remain the same.

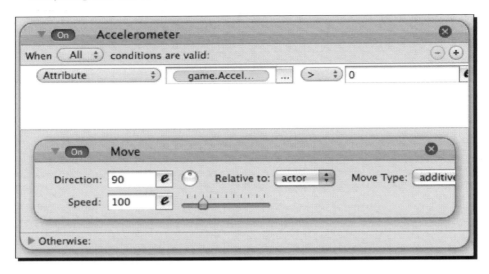

3. Now, duplicate that rule and change it from **> 0** to **< 0** and change the **Direction** to 270.

4. Create two new attributes back in the **Inspector**, both of them will be Booleans, one called Left and the other Right, very simple.

5. We have to do some more touch controls. Create two new actors, also named **Left** and **Right**. Open the **Left** one up and we are going to edit it. Change the **Size** by making the **Width** 240 and **Height** 320. Now, let's create a new rule and change it to **Actor receives event | touch | is | pressed**.

6. Then, drag in a **Change Attribute** and change it to **Change Attribute: | game.Left | To: | true**.

7. Expand the **Otherwise** roll-out, and drag in a copy of the last **Change Attribute** behavior and change it from **true** to **false**.

The settings are shown in the following screenshot:

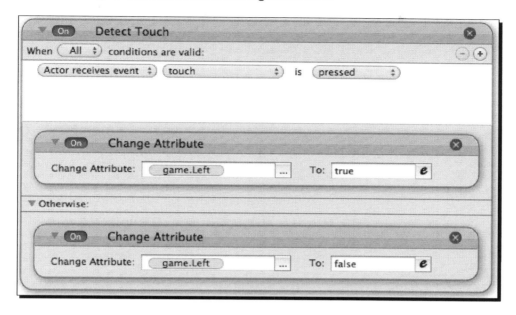

8. Finally, drag in a **Change Attribute** and change the settings to **Change Attribute: | self.Color.Alpha | To: | 0**.

This will hide the actor as soon as we hit play.

9. Now, let's go to the **Right** actor and add in the same rule and behaviors, but of course change it from **game.Left** to **game.Right**.

10. Now, let's go to our **Player** actor and in our **iPhone Movement** group, create a new rule and change it to **Attribute: | game.Left | To: | true**.

11. Now, let's drag in a **Rotate** behavior, and change the settings to the following:

- **Direction:** Counter-Clockwise
- **Speed:** 200

12. Simply duplicate that rule, change it from **game.Left** to `game.Right`, and change the **Rotate** direction to `Clockwise`, it's that easy!

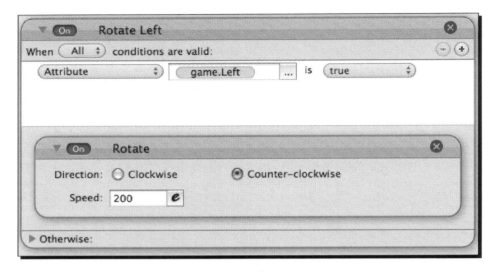

What just happened?

In this section, we looked at making our player move using the device's accelerometer. Then, we set up two Booleans that when triggered (or turned to **true**) made our player rotate left and right accordingly.

That's it for the iPhone controls! Now, we are done with the main development of the game; all you have to do from here is finish the rest of the levels.

Have a go hero

Why not try out your own type of controls, such as two thumb sticks to control and rotate the player. Not sure how to do that? Why not take a look at the **Official Cross-Platform Controller Template** in the new section of projects, examine the behaviors and give it a try.

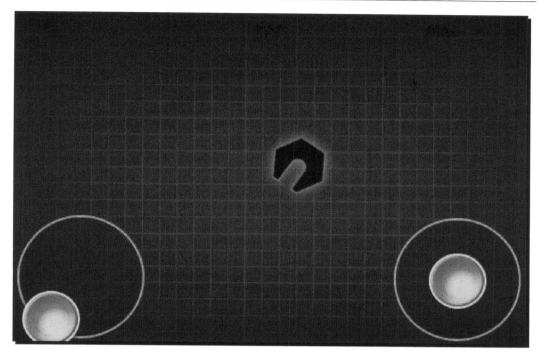

The two thumb stick controller looks something similar to the previous screenshot; it makes the gameplay much better. Some people don't like accelerometer controls, so why not give the player a choice at the beginning of the game to select accelerometer or touch controls? This would be done with a simple **boolean** attribute that will be checked through the whole game; if the Boolean is true, use tilt controls, if it's false, use touch controls. It's simple!

Now that we are done with developing the game (in terms of gameplay), in the next chapter we will be setting up the player leaderboards, testing the game on our devices, preparing the game for the App Store, and then finally deploying it for the App Store! This is where the fun begins! You are getting closer and closer to making money on your own creation. Isn't it exciting? Once you see your creation on the App Store, you are going to be so excited and then you'll see the reviews coming in, and most importantly the paychecks!

Pop quiz

1. How do you prevent an actor from moving on collision?

    a. Add in a rule that constantly sets the player's speed at 0

    b. In the **Actors** attributes under **Physics** uncheck **Moveable**

    c. Set the player's maximum speed to 0

    d. None of the above

2. True or False: You can change the actor's colors on the fly.

    a. True

    b. False

3. How do you do a multi-condition rule?

    a. You can't

    b. Add a second rule into the current rule

    c. Click the + button inside of the rule's condition

    d. None of the above

Summary

In this chapter, we looked at many core mechanics of an iPhone game. We looked at how to add in accelerometer controls, touch controls, and other game play aspects. What we learned in this chapter can be used in any type of game. Accelerometer controls are common to almost all iPhone games; as for touch controls, every iPhone game has those whether for menus or gameplay. We also looked at some critical gameplay mechanics such as collisions, NPC's (non-player characters) such as turrets and other mechs, sound effects, overheating weapons when the player keeps shooting, missions briefing within the game's user interface, and scoring. So go give it a try my friend, make a masterpiece!

11
Metal Mech Part 4

Well my friends, this is the last chapter! We have covered a lot of information regarding GameSalad and game development, but now we get to the part that every aspiring game developer looks forward to, preparing their game for deployment, selling it, and making money in various ways (aside from the app sales there's also iAd revenue).

Let's take a look at exactly what we are going to be doing in this chapter:

- Preparing your game for the App Store
- iAds
- Game Center Leaderboards
- Testing your game on a device
- Upload your game to the App Store and make money!
- Review

Putting your App on the App Store

You have come so far! Who doesn't get excited at this part? I still get excited when one of my games is released on the App Store! I just want to clarify that you aren't guaranteed to make bundles of money. Big game companies, such as the one who made Angry Birds or Cut the Rope are able to dump loads of money into advertising to get their name out there and they get noticed. Not to burst your bubble, but it's one of the biggest mistakes that individuals like you and I make when first starting out.

You think you are going to get rich and quick, but when you see you don't, or you see negative reviews, DON'T GIVE UP! It has happened to so many people, they make a game that they think will break the market as the next best thing, then when they barely make any money, or they see negative reviews they just give up, instead of seeing what they did wrong, or maybe advertising it a little bit. Ok, let's do this!

Time for action – preparing for deployment

Our game is great, but it may not work as well on the iPhone as it does on the computer. Your computer is much more powerful than the iPhone, so we may need to make some changes to our game to increase the performance on the device.

1. First off, let's open up our game again, and we are going to test our game with the **GS Viewer** app to test how it will run on the device.

2. Open up that app on your device, it doesn't matter if it is on an iPhone or an iPod Touch, just as long as it's on the same wireless network as your Mac running GameSalad.

3. Now, you will see a new button appear in GameSalad that says Preview on iPhone. When you test in GameSalad, you will see performance figures for things like frames per second and memory used by images, sounds, and so on.

4. For optimal performance, you want to keep the **Frames per second** around 32 or more. To boost performance, you may need to lower things, such as the amount of particles per emitter (for example, reducing the number of particles in an emitter from 100 to 50, which still looks good but will make a lot of difference in terms of performance), or amount of actors on the screen. At one point while I was testing my game, I saw the frame rate drop to less than 20, so I dropped the amount of particles being emitted on each actor.

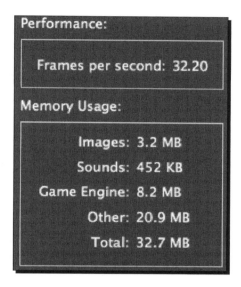

5. Now that it's running properly on our devices, we are going to integrate **Game Center** and **iAds**.

What just happened?

In this section, we tested our device using the GameSalad viewer on our phone. This gives us great insight on how our game will run on the device because GameSalad gives us all the performance figures, as shown in the previous screenshot.

Time for action – integrating Game Center and iAds

Game Center is a great, social way for users who play your game to interact with other players. Game Center includes leaderboards and achievements (which is currently not an available feature in GameSalad), plus you can also interact with other users who play the game, you can see their score and compare with yours. This social aspect makes your game more enjoyable to play (when programming you can integrate Facebook and Twitter as well). iAds is great for added revenue; by adding them into your app, you will be putting in content-rich advertisements. Best of all, you'll get paid for them!

1. Let's go to our **Main Menu** scene and double-click our **Menu Image** actor. Firstly, let's drag in a **Game Center – Login** behavior. Now, we are going to create a new actor to display the **Leaderboards**. We are going to use the same image as the **Start Button**.

2. Create a new Rule and change the settings to **Actor receives event | touch | is | pressed**.

3. Drag in a **Game Center – Show Leaderboard** behavior. Now, we have to take a break to set up our leaderboards on the Apple developer page.

4. Go to www.itunesconnect.apple.com, log in and click on **Manage Your Applications** and if you have already created your app, click on it. If not, you will have to create a new app. The following screenshot is an example of this step:

5. Now, click **Manage Game Center**, then click **Enable**, and under **Leaderboards** click **Set Up**.

6. On the next page, click **Add Leaderboard** and fill out all the info accordingly. The great thing about this is that you can add many languages for the leaderboards, so all users around the world can use it. As you see in the following screenshot, you can fill out all the information in any language you want! You can always use a free translator or if you know the language, even better!

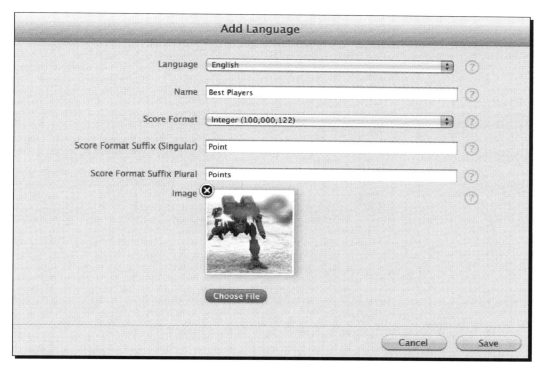

7. Ok, now, the number you set for the **Leaderboard ID**, copy that, or even write it down so that you remember it through the rest of the game.

8. Now, click **Save** and you will see your leaderboard saved, similar to the following screenshot. If you are done, let's go back to GameSalad and fill in the **Leaderboard ID**.

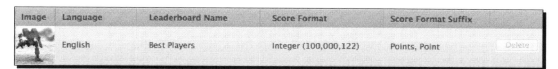

9. Next, drag in a **Display Text** behavior, change the **Text** to High Scores, the **Align** to middle, the **Font** to Futura, and the **Size** to 20.

10. At the end of each set of levels, create a screen that will show the final score for those levels, and include in that scene an actor that will post the score.

11. Now, we are going to focus on iAds. Go back to your App page on the iTunes Connect page, click on the **Set Up iAd Network**, select your target audience and then click on **Enable iAds**. Click on **Save** and go back to GameSalad.

12. These can be displayed at any time, but I'll show you how. In our **Main Menu** scene, let's click on the **Menu Image** actor, now get ready for this. It's so hard! Drag in a **Show iAd** behavior, and select the **Banner Position** and that's it! That was tough, wasn't it?

What just happened?

In this section, we easily integrated Game Center and iAds into our game. Game Center adds more playability for users because they can compare their top score with players and friends, and iAds enables content-rich advertisements to be pushed into your app, which means that you get paid for them!

When using a device for development, iAds will not be displayed. All you will get is a Test Advertisement, and when you tap it, a full screen ad will show up saying **Test Advertisement**. This confirms that test advertisements are running correctly. Also, when you are testing your game before release on iTunes, you may get an error saying that the app is not recognized by Game Center. If this happens, go into the Game Center app and log out. Then, in the app you are testing, you will get a pop-up asking you to sign in to Game Center, but you will notice that there is something new here, you will see *** Sandbox ***, this means that you are now in development mode, and you will be able to test all the Game Center abilities as if the app were released.

Publish, provision, and deploy

Now, let's publish our masterpiece! To do this, we need to publish our game in GameSalad. Then, before we deploy it to our device, we have to create and download a **Provisioning Profile**. By installing it to our device, we can deploy our game to that device.

Time for action – creating provisioning profiles, publishing in GameSalad, and deploying!

1. In GameSalad, click the **Publish** button, as shown in the following screenshot:

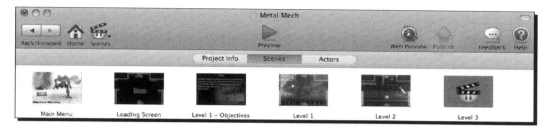

2. Now you will be asked to select the platform you want to deploy on, as you can see in the next screenshot:

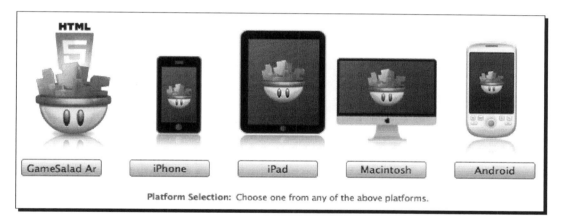

3. This whole game has been created for the iPhone (though most of it will work on Android as well), so let's click **iPhone**. Then click **Create New Game**.

 If you have already published this, just click the app, then click **Update** and skip what I'm about to say.

4. GameSalad will now ask you to fill in all the information on your game, to upload all the screenshots and stuff. Click **Next** then it will ask you to select your provisioning profile (don't forget to select the correct profile: if you are going to be testing your game on the device first, then you should use a **Development** profile; but if you are publishing your app for the App Store, then you should select the **Distribution** profile.)

5. Next, you can fill in the display name (what you will see on the device) and the version number (for updates), as shown in the following screenshot:

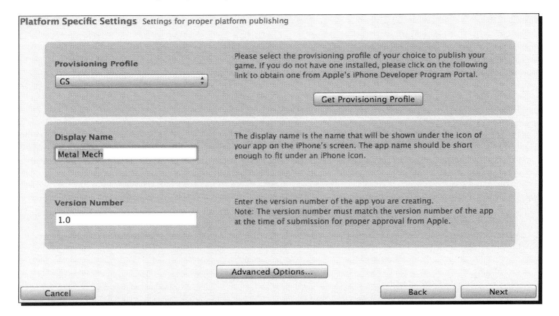

 If you do not know how to set up a provisioning profile, we are going to take a look at it in the Appendix.

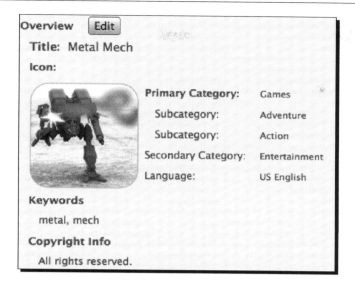

6. You will now have a chance to review everything, as shown in the previous screenshot. If it is all good, scroll down and click the **Publish** button. You will next be asked to agree to the **GameSalad Terms and Agreement**, just click **Agree and Upload**.

7. GameSalad will now upload your app to their servers, and after a while you will be asked where you want to save it. Choose anywhere you like, but pick somewhere easy enough to find again.

8. When it's all done, click the **Test** button. If that doesn't work, you can install the app through Xcode, a walkthrough for which is available in the Appendix. It is a good idea to test the final, published version of your app on your device before deploying it to the App Store, just to make sure everything still works well because sometimes the **GS Viewer** doesn't work as well as the finished product.

What just happened?

In this section, we built our app in GameSalad by using provisioning profiles, published it, and then we deployed our game to our device!

iTunes Connect

When developing apps, you will be spending a lot of time in the Apple development portal (www.developer.apple.com/iphone or www.itunesconnect.apple.com). From here, you can create your apps on Apple's servers, prepare them for release, set prices, and so on. So now, we are going to have a small guided tour of iTunes Connect, and how to create apps within it.

Time for action – deploying our app to iTunes Connect

1. Once you have finished all your testing, right-click the app and click **Compress "..."** (this being the name of the file), which will now "zip" your app. Now that the app is all done, you can close GameSalad and go to www.itunesconnect.apple.com. Log in and click **Manage Your Applications**, then on the next page, click **Add New App**. If you are signed in for multiple developer accounts for iOS and Mac, click **iOS** on the next page.

2. Change the app name to whatever you like. The **SKU** number is just a number to identify your app, I usually change it to the current time that I am uploading it, so in this case, 955, and the **Bundle ID** to the one you set up (again we discuss all of this in the appendix). Click **Continue** and you are asked to select an availability date, price, and specific stores that you want your app to show up in as shown in, the following screenshot:

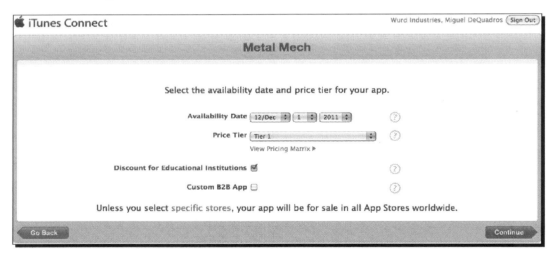

Just a note on pricing, there are 85 different price tiers all ranging from $0.99 all the way to $999.99 USD. Think carefully when you are choosing your price; if you set it too high, no one will want to buy it. Start off at $0.99, or price tier 1, then if you get little or no downloads, change it to free later. Now we have to fill out all the **Metadata**, this is all the stuff the user will see on the App Store when they download it. All of this information is very important, especially the description. You have to grab the attention of the user before he or she even looks at the screenshots. Think about what you are going to say because it can make or break your app. If it doesn't sound interesting, why will anyone buy it?

Metadata

Version Number	1.0
Description	Take control of a PACV Mech as a member of the USMA. It is 2099 and the world has been over run by a greedy crime boss who is harvesting all the worlds remaining resources for their greedy gain. The USMA has to step in and take serious action. The fate of the world rests on your shoulders, you cannot mess this up. We are all depending on you soldier!
Primary Category	Games
Subcategory	Action
Subcategory	Adventure
Secondary Category (optional)	Select
Keywords	Metal, Mech, Wurd, Industries, MigApps, Apps
Copyright	2011 Wurd Industries and MigApps
Contact Email Address	miguel@wurdindustries.com
Support URL	http://www.wurdindustries.com/contactus
App URL (optional)	http://
Privacy Policy URL (optional)	
Review Notes (optional)	

3. You will then be met with the **Metadata** screen as shown in the previous screenshot. In this page, you will be asked to fill out the version number, description, categories, keywords, copyright information, contact e-mail (customer/tech support), support URL (if you have a website set up for your app), app URL, privacy policy URL, and the review notes.

4. Now, if you scroll down you have to rate your app, not 4 out of 5 Stars, but kind of like an ESRB or PEGI rating. Rate the amount of cartoon and realistic violence, sexual content, nudity (any app with this rating may be rejected by Apple, they do not allow any games or apps with explicit nudity), profanity, crude humor, alcohol, tobacco, drug use or references, mature/suggestive themes, simulated gambling, horror/fear themes, prolonged graphic or sadistic realistic violence, graphic sexual content and nudity, these have 3 degrees of frequency: None, Infrequent/Mild, and Frequent/Intense.

5. Based on your rating, you will get 1 out of 5 ratings for your app. They are as follows:

This app can be used by children; there is almost no violence or anything offensive whatsoever in this game.

Example: Toy Tennis

This app will include mild cartoon or fantasy violence, nothing severe.

Example: iMMUNE 1, and iMMUNE 2: Rise of the Salmonella

This will be more intense, frequent violence, profanity, or horrific images that may offend users.

Example: Rage

This is pretty self-explanatory; this app will be very intense, it will include lots of graphic violence, frequent intense use of profanity, or crude humor.

Example: Hilarious Pickup Lines 17+

This app, as you can see, will not be published through iTunes, the app is so explicit or offensive, that Apple will automatically reject it.

6. The game that we have been creating is only 9+, so now let's upload it.

7. You have to upload a big icon as well, it's 512x512. This will be the main icon image that you will see on the App Store. It has to be close to the current icon that you will see on your home screen, and the one you provided in the GameSalad project when you published it, otherwise it will be rejected by Apple.

8. Next upload some screenshots, preferably some really awesome-looking ones! Click **OK** and your app will be created. Following is a screenshot of the application information screen:

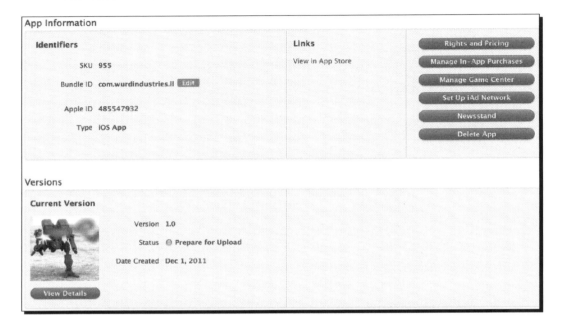

What just happened?

In this section, you got a small tour of how to create your app within iTunes Connect. This included setting the price, uploading screenshots, choosing what App stores you will deploy in, and more.

Time for action – uploading our app to iTunes Connect

By now you should have a good idea of how to create apps in iTunes, but now we have to upload our app to Apple. Let's get to that!

1. Click the **View Details** button right under the app icon on the current page, you will then be taken to the App Detail page. At the very top of this page, you will see a button that says **Ready to Upload**; click that and you will be taken to a page that will ask you if your app has any encryption, which it doesn't, so click **No** and then **Continue**.

2. From here, your app is now ready for upload. On your computer, find the **Application Loader** (again, discussed in the appendix).

 The latest version of this program is very different from what it used to be. If you are used to the old one, no worries, it's still pretty easy to use.

3. Simply click the **Deliver Your App** button, it will then check with Apple's servers to see if your app is marked as **Ready for Upload**. If it is, select it from the drop-down box, then click **Next**.

4. You will now be shown the application information. Click the **Choose...** button, find your app and select it, click **Next**, then click **Send**.

Your app will now be delivered to Apple's servers, and will be ready for review. Wait for about 1-3 weeks, depending on how busy Apple is, and you will see your app on the App Store!

 You can check the current congestion for Apple's review times at: http://reviewtimes.shinydevelopment.com/.

What just happened?

We just looked at how to upload our app to Apple's server by preparing it for upload and using Application Loader.

Setting up payment info, and checking your daily sales

So exciting, isn't it? Before you can get paid though, you must fill out all the contracts! Go back to the main page of iTunes Connect, and click the **Contracts, Tax, and Banking** link. From here, you can fill out all your banking information so that you get paid!

Well, it's been two weeks and your app is finally on the App Store! Congratulations! I bet you are excited to see how it's doing, aren't you? To see that, click the **Sales and Trends** link. From here, you will be able to see your daily updates; unfortunately, you do not get hourly ones.

FAQs about payments (because everyone wants their money!)

When are you going to get paid? Well, here is what Apple says regarding this:

Why didn't I get paid? What are the requirements?

Payments are made within 45 days of calendar month end, if both of the following conditions are met:

◆ All documentation is complete, including any required banking and tax information.

◆ The payment threshold of USD $150 has been exceeded.

If you have not received a payment for a given month within 45 days after the end of the month, please confirm that all documentation has been completed and provided. Also, please confirm that the cumulative amount owed exceeds USD $150 by converting reported amounts using current exchange rates.

I'm not going to quote all of Apple's guidelines, but if you want to, there is a plethora of documentation on the developer website.

Well, that's it for now! Where can you go from here? Anywhere! You are just touching the tip of the iceberg. GameSalad is very powerful, if you know how to use it properly. You can do very powerful complex behaviors, nothing like the ones we looked at in this book. Also, if you are feeling adventurous enough, why not try learning a programming language? There is so much that you can do when you program it, it is difficult, but it's worth it in the long run.

I really hope that you enjoyed this book. It was truly a blast to write it and I hope that I have helped you take off on your journey of game development. Just to check that I have, it's quiz time! Good luck my friend!

Pop quiz

1. What is the preferred frame rate for games?

    a. 32

    b. 29

    c. 60

    d. 100

2. How many price tiers are there for selling your app?

    a. 17

    b. 85

    c. 90

    d. 210

3. True or False: Your app will be rejected if you have nudity in it

    a. True, no app can have nudity in it

    b. False, some apps are rated for nudity, but it depends on the app

4. How do you upload your app?

    a. With your app marked as **Ready for Upload**, open the **Application Loader** to upload

    b. In the iTunes Connect website, click the **Upload** button to upload it

    c. You e-mail your app to `connect@apple.itunes.com`

    d. None of the above

5. What file format does Apple accept for uploads?

    a.   *.zip

    b.   *.rar

    c.   *.tar

    d.   *.app

Summary

In this book, you have gradually learned how to build your own awesome iOS game. This book has not only taught you how to create your own funky iPhone game, but you can also use what you learned to deploy your game to the Mac App Store, or even to the Android Market. By now, you can build a relatively complex game with almost any feature you would like! You know how to incorporate touch controls, acceleration controls, Game Center integration, iAds, and more. Don't forget that GameSalad is still being updated on a regular basis with newer and greater features all the time. I hear they may add Game Center achievements (which would be completely fantastic), ability to use videos within your app (which is one feature I have been dying to have) and more. GameSalad is amazing and I definitely recommend it to anyone who dreams about creating their own game, but who cannot spare the time, effort and headaches to learn a programming language. Have a ball my friends! Good luck in all your efforts, and I hope that I have taught you well.

Getting Started in iDevelopment

For this whole book I have been discussing things that I assume you already know about, such things as provisioning, deploying, and so on; things that are not part of GameSalad but are an integral part of iOS development. In this appendix, we are going to discuss some of the very basics of iOS development, things such as:

- ◆ Becoming a registered developer
- ◆ Downloading Xcode
- ◆ Code Signing and Provisioning Profiles
- ◆ App Loader

Becoming a registered developer

Following is a screenshot, which shows the screen after registration:

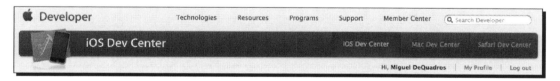

First off, let's start with becoming a registered developer, go to `www.developer.apple.com`, scroll down, and find the section that says **Join the iOS Developer Program** and click on it.

On the next page, you will see a button at the top that says **Enroll Now** for $99/year, this is the standard rate for individual developers, as shown in the following screenshot:

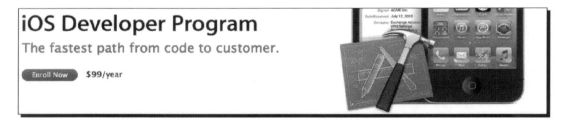

The important fine print for business owners at the bottom states:

"***Business Requirements: The person enrolling on behalf of the company or organization must have the legal authority to bind his or her company to any legal agreements that may be presented during the enrolment process or membership year. This person may also need to provide business documents including, but not limited to Articles of Incorporation, Business License, etc. as part of our identity verification process. Technical Requirements: You must have an Intel-based Mac running Mac OS X Snow Leopard or later to develop and distribute iOS and Mac OS X apps.**"

You cannot sign up as a Business with Sole Proprietorship; if you select this, you will be spending about five days e-mailing Apple only to find out that they cannot process your request because you do not meet the Business account requirements. So, for now, we are just going to sign up as an individual.

On the next page, you will be asked to either use your previous Apple ID, or to create a new one. If you have one sign in, if you don't, you can create one right now. You will next be asked if you want to create an **Individual** or a **Business** account. Let's choose **Individual**. Now, all you have to do is fill in your information, pay for it, and wait for the e-mail from Apple saying your account is active. After that, go to www.developer.apple.com/iphone and log in, then scroll down and download Xcode, as shown in the following screenshot. You will need this to install the GameSalad Viewer app on to your phone.

Provisioning and installing apps

If you are still on the iOS Dev Center page, locate the navigation bar on the side, and find the button that says **iOS Provisioning Portal**. Click on it.

You will now be taken to the Provisioning Portal; from here, you can create development profiles and distribution profiles. The first thing you are going to do is click the **Certificates** button on the side bar, and create your own Certificate. To do this, follow the following guide:

To request an iOS Development Certificate, you first need to generate a Certificate Signing Request (CSR) utilizing the Keychain Access application in Mac OS X Leopard. The creation of a CSR will prompt Keychain Access to simultaneously generate your public and private key pair, establishing your iOS Developer identity. Your private key is stored in the login Keychain by default, and can be viewed in the Keychain Access application under the 'Keys' category. To generate a CSR:

This is going to get pretty technical. If you are having a hard time following it then slow down, take your time. Once all this is set up, you won't have to do it again (at least not until your developer certificates expire, which is usually after one year)

1. In your `Applications` folder, open the `Utilities` folder and launch **Keychain Access**.

2. In the **Preferences** menu, set **Online Certificate Status Protocol (OSCP)** and **Certificate Revocation List (CRL)** to **Off**, as shown in following screenshot:

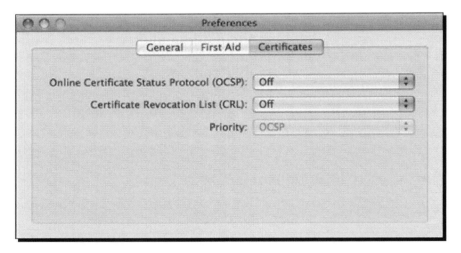

3. Choose **Keychain Access | Certificate Assistant | Request a Certificate from a Certificate Authority...**.

 If you have a noncompliant private key highlighted in the Keychain during this process, the resulting Certificate Request will not be accepted by the Provisioning Portal.

4. Confirm that you are selecting **Request a Certificate From a Certificate Authority...** and not selecting **Request a Certificate From a Certificate Authority with <Private Key>...**. Look at the following screenshot to see what I mean:

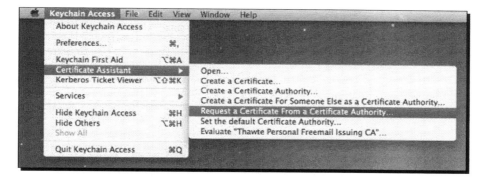

5. In the **User Email Address** field, enter your e-mail address. Please ensure that the e-mail address entered matches the information that was submitted when you registered as an iOS Developer.

6. In the **Common Name** field, enter your name. Please make sure the name you entered matches the information that was submitted when you registered as an iOS Developer.

7. Next, you will see that a **No CA (Certificate Authority) Email Address is Required**. The **Required** message will be removed after completing the following step.

8. Select the **Saved to Disk** radio button and if prompted, select **Let me specify key pair information** and click **Continue**.

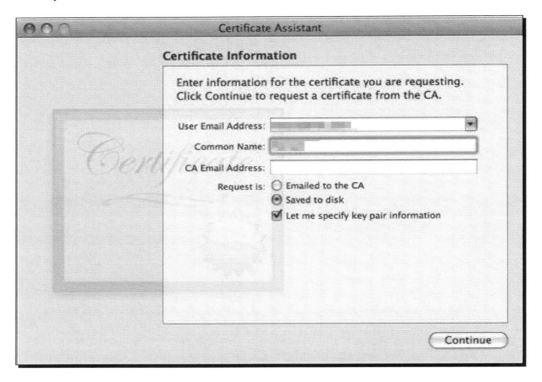

9. If **Let me specify key pair** was selected (as shown in the previous screenshot), specify a filename and click **Save**. In the following screen, select `2048 bits` for the **Key Size** and `RSA` for the **Algorithm**. Click **Continue**.

10. The Certificate Assistant will create a CSR file on your desktop.

Submitting our signing request certificate

Now, we have to submit the certificate that we just created; from here on everything should be smooth sailing. Following is what we have to do:

1. After creating a CSR (Certificate Signing Request), log in to the iOS Provisioning Portal, navigate to **Certificates | Development**, and click **Add Certificate**.

2. Click the **Choose file** button, select your CSR and click **Submit**. If the Key Size was not set to 2048 bits during the CSR creation process, the Portal will reject the CSR.

3. Upon submission, Team Admins will be notified via e-mail of the certificate request. (The way that we set up our account, you are the Team Admin. You can have numerous team admins on your account, but we won't worry about this).

4. Once your CSR is approved or rejected by a Team Admin (you), you will be notified via e-mail of the change in your certificate status.

5. Team Agents and Team Admins have the authority and responsibility to approve or reject all iOS Development Certificate requests. In order to approve/reject Team Members' requests, all Team Admins should first submit their own CSR for approval.

6. After submitting a CSR for approval, you will be directed to the **Development** tab of the **Certificates** section. Under this tab, the certificates can be approved or rejected by clicking the **Approve** or **Reject** buttons next to each request.

7. Once a certificate is approved or rejected, the requesting Team Member (which again in this case is you) is notified via e-mail of the change in their certificate status. Each iOS Development Certificate is available to both the Team Member who submitted the CSR for approval and to the Team Admin(s).

Just to clarify everything, in this case, because you are the sole owner of the developer profile, you are the Team Member and Team Admin. You will be the one who is requesting all profiles and certificates, and you will be the only one who will accept or reject any profiles (that is unless you have more than one developer on your profile, then you can set them as a Team Member or Admin).

Downloading and installing your certificate

Now, it's time for us to make use of the certificate we created, we are going to install it on our computer.

1. In the **Certificates | Distribution** section of the Developer Portal, right-click the **WWDR Intermediate Certificate** link and select **Saved Linked File to Downloads** to download the certificate.

2. On your computer, double-click the **WWDR Intermediate certificate** to launch Keychain Access program, which will then install the certificate.

3. Upon certificate approval, Team Members and Team Admins can download their certificates via the **Certificates** section of the Provisioning Portal. Click **Download** next to the certificate name to download your iOS Development Certificate to your local machine.

4. On your Mac, double-click the downloaded `.cer` file to launch Keychain Access and install your certificate (the same as done previously, but this is your personal certificate).

5. Team Members can only download their own iOS Development Certificates. Team Admins have the authority to download the public certificates of all their Team Members. Apple never receives the private key for a Certificate Signing Request. The private keys are not available to anyone except the original creator and are stored in the system keychain of that Team Member.

That's all for that part, it's a bit of a long and technical process but it is required. Now that it's done, we can proceed to adding your device, so click the **Device** button on the side bar, and do the following:

Adding your device to the Development Portal

The **Devices** section of the iOS Provisioning Portal allows you to enter the Apple devices that you will be using for your iOS development. In order to debug your iOS application on an Apple device, a Team Agent or Team Admin must first enter the Unique Device Identifier (UDID) for each iPhone and iPod Touch into the Provisioning Portal. The UDID is a 40 character string that is tied to a single device, similar to a serial number. These UDIDs are included in the provisioning profiles created later. You can input up to 100 devices for your development team.

To find out your device's UDID, simply connect your device to your Mac and open Xcode. In Xcode, navigate to the **Window** drop-down menu and select **Organizer**. The 40 hex character string in the **Identifier** field is your device's UDID, as shown in the following screenshot. Team Members should send this string to their Team Admins for input into the Provisioning Portal.

 Alternately, you can connect your device and open iTunes, click on your device in the side bar. For the iPhone, click your **Phone Number** once, it will change to your **IMEI**, then click it again and it will display your **UDID**.

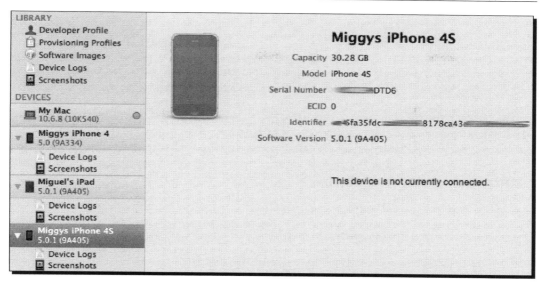

1. Upon receiving a UDID, go to the **Devices** section of the Provisioning Portal and click **Add Device**. Admins will enter a device name as well as the UDID and click '**Submit**'.

2. Connect your device to your Mac, close iTunes and launch Xcode.

3. Once Xcode detects the device, select **Use for Development** when prompted.

That's it for the devices. As mentioned earlier, you can have up to 100 devices on your account. Beware, there are many websites that you can pay to add your device to their developer profile so you can access all the beta software, this is illegal! As the warning shows in the following screenshot:

 Important: Your iOS Developer Program membership can be terminated if you provide pre-release Apple Software to anyone other than employees, contractors, and members of your organization who are registered as Apple Developers and have a demonstrable need to know or use Apple Software in order to develop and test applications on your behalf. Unauthorized distribution of Apple Confidential Information (including pre-release Apple Software) is prohibited and may subject you to both civil and criminal liability.

YIKES! You may be subject to a criminal and civil liability and I don't think any one would want that to happen.

Now let's move on to App ID's

An **App ID** is a unique identifier that iOS uses to allow your application to connect to the Apple Push Notification service, share keychain data between applications, and communicate with external hardware accessories you wish to pair your iOS application with. In order to install your application on an iOS-based device, you will need to create an App ID.

Each App ID consists of a unique 10 character "Bundle Seed ID" prefix generated by Apple, and a "Bundle Identifier" suffix that is entered by a Team Admin in the Provisioning Portal. The recommended practice is to use a reversed domain-name-style string for the "Bundle Identifier" portion of the App ID. An example App ID using this approach would be: 8E549T7128.com.apple.AddressBook.

If you are creating a suite of applications that will share the same Keychain access (for example, sharing passwords between applications) or have no Keychain Access requirements, you can create a single App ID for your entire application suite utilizing a trailing asterisk as a wildcard character. The wildcard character must be the last character in the App ID string. Example of an App ID for this situation could be: R2T24EVAEE.com. domainname. or R2T24EVAEE.

Creating an App ID

For this section, navigate to the **App ID** section of the Provisioning Portal.

1. Click **Add ID**.

2. Enter a common name for your App ID. This is a name for easy reference and identification within the Provisioning Portal.

3. Enter a Bundle Identifier in the free-form text field. The recommended usage is a reversed domain-name-style string, for example, com.domainname. applicationname. For a suite of applications sharing the same Keychain access, you should use a wildcard character in the Bundle Identifier (for example, com. domainname.* or *). This Bundle Identifier will need to match whatever CF Bundle Identifier you use for your application in Xcode.

4. Click **Submit**. At this time, the 10 character Bundle Seed ID is generated and concatenated with the Bundle Identifier you entered. This resulting string is your App ID. Note: The Bundle Seed ID does not need to be entered into Xcode.

Finally onto provisioning profiles (development only)

Ok, so that was a really long and confusing section. Don't worry, it's not something you have to do every time you want to create a new provisioning profile, that's just the initial set up. Now let's finish setting up the provisioning profile.

1. In the **Provisioning** section of the Portal, click **Add** on the **Development** tab.

2. Enter a name for the provisioning profile.

3. Specify which devices will be associated with the provisioning profile. You must specify a device in order for that device to use the provisioning profile. If a device's UDID is not included, the profile and your application cannot be installed on that device.

4. Specify which Development Certificates will be associated with the provisioning profile. You must specify an iOS Development Certificate in order for the application code signed with that same certificate to run on the device.

5. Choose a single App ID for the Development Provisioning Profile. Each Development Provisioning Profile can specify only one application ID. If you have applications requiring different Keychain access, you will need to create a separate Development Provisioning Profile for each of these applications. If you are installing a suite of applications with the same required Keychain access, or have a set of applications not requiring access to the Keychain, use an App ID containing the wildcard asterisk character to build all of your applications.

6. Click **Submit** to generate your Development Provisioning Profile.

7. You can now download a Development Provisioning Profile from the **Provisioning** section of the Portal after it has been created. Only those developers whose Apple device IDs and iOS Development Certificates are included in the provisioning profile will be able to install and test their application on their device.

8. In the **Provisioning** section of the Provisioning Portal, click the **Download** button next to the desired provisioning profile.

9. Drag the downloaded file onto the Xcode application icon in the dock or into the **Organizer** window within Xcode. This will automatically copy the `.mobileprovision` file to the proper directory. Alternatively, you can drag the `.mobileprovision` file onto the iTunes icon in the dock or copy the file to `~/Library/MobileDevice/Provisioning Profiles`. If the directory does not exist, you will need to create it. Click on the **+** button in the **Provisioning** section of the **Organizer** window to install your `.mobileprovision` file.

 Alternately, you can simply double-click the new provisioning profile and it will be automatically installed. Much easier, right? Apple's documentation always does things in a very confusing way.

Building your app and install it using your provisioning profile

Follow the given steps to build and install your app:

1. Launch Xcode and open your project; for this, let's open up the **GS Viewer** app.

2. In the **Project** window, select **Device - iPhone OS** from the **Device | Debug** drop-down menu in the upper left-hand corner.

3. Highlight the project target and select the **Info** icon from the top menu bar.

4. In the **Target Info** window, navigate to the **Build** pane and click the **Any iOS Device** pop-up menu below the **Code Signing Identity** field, then select the iOS Development Certificate/Provisioning Profile pair you wish to sign and install your code with. Your iOS Development certificate will be in bold with the Provisioning Profile associated with it in gray above. In this example, **iOS Developer: Team Leader** is the Development Certificate and **My First Development Provisioning Profile** is the `.mobileprovision` file paired with it.

5. If the private key for your iOS Development certificate is missing, or if your iOS Development certificate is not included in a provisioning profile, you will be unable to select the iOS Development Certificate/Provisioning Profile pair and you will see the following:

    Re-installing the private key or downloading a provisioning profile with your iOS Development certificate included in it will correct this.

6. In the **Properties** pane of the **Target Info** window, enter the Bundle Identifier portion of your App ID. If you have used an explicit App ID, you must enter the Bundle Identifier portion of the App ID in the Identifier field. For example, I would enter `com.wurdindustries.GSviewer`.

7. Click **Build and Go** to install the application on your Apple device.

That's all you need to do for development profiles. You can do the same with distribution profiles, but an app built with one cannot be installed on your device.

Get your app on the App Store!

As we mentioned in *Chapter 11, Metal Mech Part 4* under the *Uploading our App to iTunes Connect* heading, if your app is all ready for upload, you went through adding a new application in the iTunes Connect (`www.iTunesConnect.Apple.com`) page, and you have marked your app **Waiting For Upload**, you can now upload it using the **App Loader** application found on your computer (`/Developer/Applications/Utilities/ Application Loader.app`). You will see the icon as in the following screenshot.

1. Click the **Deliver Your App** button and a new window will open up (see the following screenshot). First it will check for available apps that are marked as **Waiting for Upload**.

2. Once it is finished, it will show you a list of apps (as shown in the following screenshot) that you can upload.

3. Click the **Next** button. On the next screen you will see your app information page (as shown in the following screenshot), this just helps you verify all your information before you upload the app. Click the **Choose...** button.

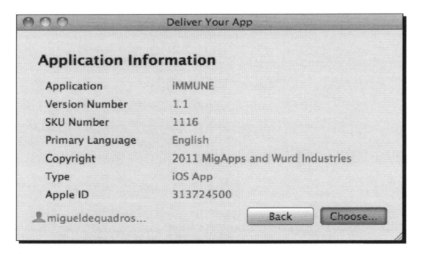

You may run into certain errors when trying to upload things such as invalid provisioning profile or invalid version number. These things are simple to fix, usually you selected the wrong provisioning profile, or the version number is different on the App than the one you specified in iTunes Connect.

4. Click the **ellipsis...** button to replace the current file before submitting.

5. Click **Send**; Application Loader will now begin submitting your app to the App Store.

6. Your app has now been delivered to Apple, wait for 1-2 weeks and you will see it on the App Store! The following screenshot is an example of an app on the App Store:

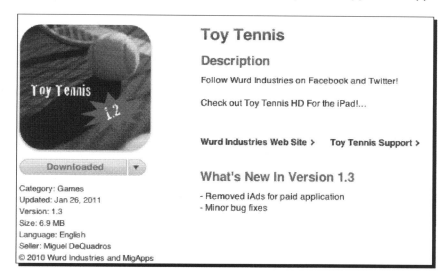

If you need any more information the Apple Documentation is always very helpful, and if something didn't work properly you can always contact the Apple Developer Support Hot Line and the people there are very helpful and will help you as much as they can. Go get 'em tiger!

B
Pop Quiz Answers

Chapter 1, You Need a Plan!

1	c
2	d
3	a

Chapter 2, Getting Started with GameSalad

1	b
2	c
3	b

Chapter 3, Add Zest to your Salad

1	c
2	d
3	d

Chapter 5, Starting Simple: Ball Drop Part 2

1	c
2	c
3	a

Chapter 6, Space Defender Part 1

1	b
2	a
3	b

Chapter 7, Space Defender Part 2

1	a
2	a
3	d

Chapter 8, Metal Mech Part 1

1	b
2	a
3	d

Chapter9, Metal Mech Part 2

1	a
2	a
3	b

Chapter 10, Metal Mech Part 3

1	b
2	a
3	c

Chapter 11, Metal Mech Part 4

1	a
2	b
3	b
4	a
5	a

Index

Thank you for buying
GameSalad Beginner's Guide

About Packt Publishing

Packt, pronounced 'packed', published its first book "Mastering phpMyAdmin for Effective MySQL Management" in April 2004 and subsequently continued to specialize in publishing highly focused books on specific technologies and solutions.

Our books and publications share the experiences of your fellow IT professionals in adapting and customizing today's systems, applications, and frameworks. Our solution-based books give you the knowledge and power to customize the software and technologies you're using to get the job done. Packt books are more specific and less general than the IT books you have seen in the past. Our unique business model allows us to bring you more focused information, giving you more of what you need to know, and less of what you don't.

Packt is a modern, yet unique publishing company, which focuses on producing quality, cutting-edge books for communities of developers, administrators, and newbies alike. For more information, please visit our website: www.PacktPub.com.

Writing for Packt

We welcome all inquiries from people who are interested in authoring. Book proposals should be sent to author@packtpub.com. If your book idea is still at an early stage and you would like to discuss it first before writing a formal book proposal, contact us; one of our commissioning editors will get in touch with you.

We're not just looking for published authors; if you have strong technical skills but no writing experience, our experienced editors can help you develop a writing career, or simply get some additional reward for your expertise.

Game Maker 8 Cookbook

ISBN: 978-1-84969-062-1   Paperback:346 pages

Over 100 recipes for quickly enhancing your game

1. Use Game Maker's simple Drag & Drop to add features to your games.

2. Enhance the complexity of your games using the Game Maker Language.

3. Apply these recipes to virtually any type of game, including 3D and online games!

4. Simple, well explained recipes designed for game maker enthusiasts at all levels.

Google SketchUp for Game Design: Beginner's Guide

ISBN: 978-1-84969-134-5   Paperback: 270 pages

Create 3D game worlds complete with textures, levels, and props

1. Learn how to create realistic game worlds with Google's easy 3D modeling tool

2. Populate your games with realistic terrain, buildings, vehicles and objects

3. Import to game engines such as Unity 3D and create a first person 3D game simulation

4. Learn the skills you need to sell low polygon 3D objects in game asset stores

Please check **www.PacktPub.com** for information on our titles

Panda3D 1.7 Game Developer's Cookbook

ISBN: 978-1-84951-292-3   Paperback:336 pages

Over 80 recipes for developing 3D games with Panda3D a full-scale 3D game engine

1. Dive into the advanced features of the Panda3D engine

2. Take control of the renderer and use shaders to create stunning graphics

3. Give your games a professional look using special effects and post-processing filters

4. Extend the core engine libraries using C++

Unreal Development Kit Beginner's Guide

ISBN: 978-1-84969-052-2   Paperback: 244 pages

A fun, quick, step-by-step guide to level design and creating your own game world

1. Full of illustrations, diagrams, and tips for creating your first level and game environment.

2. Clear step-by-step instructions and fun practical examples.

3. Master the essentials of level design and environment creation

Please check **www.PacktPub.com** for information on our titles

Made in the USA
Lexington, KY
12 June 2013